# CONTENTS

*In the book of Zen,*
*the student asked the Master:*
*"What is the greatest of the*
*wonders of the world?"*


*"The greatest wonder,"*
*answered the Master,*
*"is your consciousness*
*of these wonders."*

# DEDICATION

This book is dedicated to:

• my father Criste Jara and my mother Rosario Cazenas Jara, the two most important people in my life. Although they never had the opportunity to leave their place of birth and travel throughout this remarkable planet, by vigorously encouraging me to excel in my educational pursuits, they have paved the way which opened doors for me to visit these numerous places. May God bless them with eternal happiness;

• all those who would have loved to travel but could not;

• those who have no love for travel but will hopefully be encouraged by what they read in this book;

• those who have traveled and perhaps will gain insights from this book;

• my constant traveling companions: my daughter Maria Araceli (Bamba) Masaoy, and my friends Estela Pelayo, Willy Pelayo, Bel Canosa, Nelia Beaman, Marilou Verzosa and Irene Salazar; and to my not-so-constant companions, but nevertheless wonderful fellow travelers Leo Yjares, Carrie Goze, Connie Tolentino, my sister Elena Jara, and many others. Their companionship makes every trip extraordinarily memorable;

• my daughter Rosanne who gives me peace of mind during my frequent travels;

• God the Almighty, the supreme power over all creation!

# ACKNOWLEDGEMENTS

During the Holy Mass on the last day of our recent (2010) pilgrimage to the Holy Land, our spiritual guide, Father Alex Barbieto, requested each one of us to say aloud our petitions and thanks to God. One of our traveling companions, Bob Ruelo, who often expresses his prayers in a long litany, ended that day's petition with, "May the Holy Spirit guide Evelyn when she writes the journal of this pilgrimage." I was so touched by his thoughtful prayer and I believe that the prayer was answered by the inspiration to write, not just the day-to-day pilgrimage journal, but this particular book. I thank God for Bob!

Never could I have done this work without the invaluable help and encouragement of a dear friend, Mr. Norman S. Karpf, a famous New Jersey certified civil trial attorney who is admitted to practice before the United States Supreme Court. He is also a prominent author and lecturer. His scholarly knowledge and comprehensive insights were extremely beneficial. He skillfully and meticulously edited my work. I thank God for Mr. Karpf!

Without my friends and colleagues Leo Yjares and Estela Pelayo, who organized our travels, I would not have been able to reach the far corners of the globe which gave rise to the insightful experiences written herein. I thank God for Leo and Estela.

To enhance the presentation of this book, my brilliant thirteen-year-old granddaughter Kiara selected appropriate photographs from the numerous photo collections which my fellow travelers and I shared. She also rendered indispensable technical input. I thank God for Kiara!

The cover was artfully designed by my son, Jose. I thank God for Jose!

Without God's creation of this beautiful and wondrous world which we live in, love, and admire, this endeavor would not have been possible. I thank you, God!

"*The world is a book, and those who do not travel read only a page.*"

*St. Augustine*

# PROLOGUE

To put the contents of this book in the proper perspective, I must begin by mentioning my roots. I was born, reared, raised and grew up in a quiet, tiny, poor, rural and insignificant corner of the globe where everyone knew everybody else. The geographical smallness of the town was, to me, a huge restricting factor which limited our opportunities. Nevertheless, I am proud of my town. It is here where complete freedom came hand in hand with the simplicity of life. There was freedom to roam the countryside without any fear of being run over by vehicles ... there were too few of them; without fear of child molesters or kidnappers ... they were unheard of; without fear of bullies ... everyone respected each other; without fear of being discriminated against because of one's ethnicity, race, religion or economic status ... we were a truly homogeneous community; without fear of robbers and porch climbers ... there were none of those; without fear of celebrating the Christian festivities in cooperation with civic leaders ... religious and civil obedience came hand in hand. Unfortunately, there was no freedom from want. Most incomes came from seasonal farm products; food was scarce; medical services were a rarity.

Although occasionally I visited the city where my paternal grandparents lived, that, too, was a small city. Had I not left my town for the nation's capital city of Manila and the adjacent Quezon City where my parents sent me for my studies at the university; had I not flown farther out to the other corners of the globe, my world would have been confined and restricted. My "tiny patch of earth" would not have expanded. I would not have experienced nor learned lessons which a wider and more diverse world has offered.

Suffice it to say, despite the many fruitful benefits of international travel, I continue to have enormous respect and unending reverence for my roots, namely the wonderful little community of Dao, Antique, Philippines, where I was fortunate enough to truly learn the real meaning of life. My past will always be an integral source of pride and gratitude within me.

My simple beginnings provided me with the sensitivity to grasp the central theme and inner meaning of my numerous reactions to both remarkable sights and subtle nuances experienced during my journeys. They have allowed me to have a deeper understanding and intense appreciation of the complexities that abound on this vast earth.

America, to me, is the door, the window, and the bridge to the rest of the world. Since I immigrated to this venerable country in 1989, I have traveled extensively both within and outside of the USA: a lifelong dream come true.

At one point during my citizenship interview, the interviewing officer curiously eyed the multitude of exit and re-entry stamps on my passport. She handed it back to me and said, "Now you can travel more easily to as many more countries as you wish ... with a few exceptions, of course!" To me, those words seemed to say, "Go, travel and see God's creation in the beauty of nature, man's achievements in the past and the present, as well as man's inhumanity to man in some areas devastated by war!" That sentiment may not have been what she truly meant, but I took the liberty to interpret it as such. ... And why not?

I think of travel in three dimensions: travel **to places,** travel **in time,** and travel **through life.**

Travel to a lot of interesting places. ... I sure did ... I still do ... and God-willing, hope to do more. During these trips I have not only immensely enjoyed the experiences. I have "filled up my senses" for I have seen, touched, felt, heard, tasted something new all the time. And I have learned ... a great deal, if I may say so.

I have always traveled in the company of friends and relatives for I believe that being with them makes the trip more enjoyable and meaningful. Happiness shared has a multiplicative effect that lives on forever!

Travel in time. ... These are what memories are made of. These are what memoirs are written for. I look back and see the changes around me. I realize I am in it, sometimes with it, other times against it.

Travel through life: through the drudgery of the daily routine, through the joys and successes, through the happiness and pains, through the difficulties and struggles, through all its twists and turns, through its ups and downs. ... This, too, I have been doing, I still do and I will continue doing for as long as I live.

I have learned much from these experiences. I have learned from the mistakes I have committed and the mistakes of those with whom I traveled. Some of these were due to ignorance or sheer stupidity; some due to innocence or naivete. Some were funny, and others were not. Some were nearly tragic.

There is, however, magic in these mistakes. They somehow imbed themselves indelibly in the human psyche ... they are clearly remembered. Either we keep them there to torture ourselves with remorse and shame or we turn them into comical moments, laugh at them and ourselves, and above all, use them as teaching / learning experiences. I have chosen the latter.

Then there are those unexpectedly heartwarming incidents, when the kindness of strangers become events to be celebrated. These, too, are what we find as we travel through life literally and figuratively.

Then there are those unusual events that boggle the mind, warm the heart, display the greatness of humanity and the lovely simplicity of ordinary folks. And there are those places which pour forth the magnificent beauty which only God can create. All these and much more make up the tapestry sewn together in a traveler's mind.

These experiences and thoughts are what I would want so very much to share with the reader. I am sharing with you fragments of my travels to places, portions of my travels through life, and caplets of my travels in time.

If what you read in this book brings forth from you a chuckle, a smile, a grin, a bit of laughter, a tear, a raised eyebrow, or some new and deeper insight into certain ordinary or extraordinary events, then this book would have done what it was written for.

# TRAVELING ON THE WINGS OF DREAMS

A beach near my childhood home

Igcaputol Beach is about one mile from the Dao Catholic High School campus. Every once in a while we high schoolers would walk to the beach for the simple pleasures of walking together, breathing the salty air, flying kites, picking up seashells and stones, playing with the waves or simply walking barefoot on the sand and romping around the way teenagers do. That was during the mid-to-late fifties.

I remember how, as a young girl, I sat on a rock at that beach, looked across the endless ocean, watched the sun set over the horizon and contemplated. "What could be lying yonder on the other edge?" I dreamed for answers. I did not want the answers to come from the pages of a book. I wanted to fly over to where this seemingly endless expanse of water ended on the other side. If only I could fly on the wings of my dreams, then there would have been no problem.

Inch by inch, through the years, unknowingly I was getting nearer to where I dreamed I'd be. Prayer after prayer, labors, sweat, determination, hope ... all these worked together.

Three and a half decades later I flew to California. There I found another edge of a wide expanse of water. This was the Pacific Ocean, far across from Igcaputol Beach where, in the distant past, I dreamed for answers.

Fate had it that I found myself later in New Jersey. Like an old movie rewinding, I sat at the Jersey shore and contemplated.

"What could be lying yonder on the other edge?" This time it didn't take too long for the answer to unfold. I flew to England, Portugal, Spain. Then I knew what was on the other side of the Atlantic Ocean, far across from the Jersey shore.

No longer do I ask these questions. I know what is on both sides of some of the seemingly endless seas. Just as I've seen both sides of the oceans of my dreams: the Pacific and the Atlantic, I have also seen both sides of the China Sea, the Baltic Sea, the Dead Sea, the Sea of Galilee, the Black Sea and the Mediterranean Sea.

All of these started with a flight on the wings of a prayer and a dream.

Lesson learned: *"Let your visions go beyond the horizon; let the wings of your prayers and dreams fly you to distant shores. Chances are, reality will follow."*

# THE JOURNEY BEGINS
## (A Tribute to my Parents)

A typical Philippine rural scene. Note the
nipa hut and coconut palm trees

Every journey has a beginning. Mine started in a nipa hut surrounded by coconut palm trees where an otherwise peaceful existence was intermittently shattered by bombs bursting in air and
a call for people to duck into ditches. There I started my journey
with an extraordinary woman and an equally extraordinary man
who gave me life and nurtured me.

I was truly blest. Rosario Cazenas and Criste Jara, my mother
and father, were there to jumpstart and lead me through my journey.
Together their simple, serene, almost effortless approach to life despite the devastation left behind by the Second World War left its
mark on me. They went through life with "grace under pressure".

Although my father did not finish high school, the talent that
he inherently had was shown in the quality of life he lived and in
his humble achievements. He was the most honest and the most
honorable person I have known in my life. His integrity was beyond question. He was well respected and loved by everyone in
his adopted town. His generosity was beyond doubt. In his humility, he bore the dignity worthy of a noble man. That was the kind
of wealth he gathered. To me these qualities are the true and most
unbiased measure of a man's stature and greatness.

He was loving to his family. He wanted to bestow upon us the
best he could offer ... and through hard work ... and by the sweat
of their brows, he and my mother did.

My parents were not wealthy. But neither were we destitute. Right after the Second World War, my parents courageously opened a small store in front of our bamboo and nipa house in the southern part of town. Because of their diligence and hard work, what started as a tiny general store grew into an entrepreneurial business. Because of my father's training as a pharmacy clerk at his sister's pharmacy in the city, he was able to get a permit to open up his own pharmacy in Dao. Thus began the first pharmacy in town.

I remember that store, a little rectangular building in front of our house, a house which in the 1950's was changed into a semi-permanent residential structure. My parents were so happy and proud as they watched the carpenters nail down a huge sign in front of the store. It read: Farmacia Jara.

Truth is, the pharmacy was only a part of the store. In this little store you could buy anything from needles to nails, nuts and bolts, plows, hankies or dress materials, ice cold soda or kerosene, rice or mongo beans, as well as honey, coffee, sugar, cortal, aspirin, elixir paregoric, mercurochrome and antibiotics. Then on the next lot you could fill up your car or your truck with Shell gasoline. If you needed to mill your rice after harvest, my father was ready with his four-wheeled rice mill to go to where your dried husked rice (palay) was to be worked on. If you needed to go to the city, my father had his truck and driver to drive you there.

If you were new to the town and needed a place to eat or to sleep (Needless to say, hotels nor inns were unheard of in such a rural area.), my parents, who were the most hospitable people in town, always kept our doors open to strangers. Not only did they accommodate the stranger; they offered him the best of what they had. This was where I learned to set the table with the proper table cloth, dinner plates, a complete set of utensils, napkins, coasters and drinking glasses ... like they did at my grandfather's mansion in the city. Strangers were welcomed by my parents as if they were visiting royalty.

Perhaps subconsciously to honor Christ, his namesake, Christmas was the most special day for my father. While everyone else in town went back to sleep after the Midnight Mass on Christmas

Eve, my father always saw to it that we celebrated Christ's birthday with a gathering of friends and relatives at table in a festive Noche Buena. This is a tradition that we still hold dear.

In this tiny rural town where I grew up, people had extraordinarily conservative emotions. My mother was not the kissy-kissy, huggy-huggy type. We were called by our nicknames but never with the sweetie-honey-sweetheart-darling-love-you kind of funny names. That was the norm in my home. We were comfortable with it and we did not ask for more.

There was a significant custom which stands out in my memory. At dusk all of us children filed past our father and mother, took their hands and gently touched them to our foreheads. This was a form of blessing which they gave with much pleasure. That was the moment of the day when love seemed to envelop all of us.

As a young girl, I didn't realize anything extraordinary about my mother ... not until I grew up and started to understand a little more about life. A few of the many incidents involving her now come back to memory. I stand in awe when I remember them.

It was two o'clock in the morning. Our town was pitch black. A tiny stream of light coming from a flashlight pierced through the darkness hitting the bamboo slats which covered the windows for the night. My parents' bedroom was about four feet from the street. Our neighbors knew exactly how to wake my parents up.

"Mrs. Jara, Mrs. Jara, my little son ... he ... he's burning with fever." A panic-stricken neighbor was calling out for help. Lourdes, a laid back stocky middle-aged woman, desperately needed some medication for her infant child. Hearing her frightened screams in the wee hours of the morning truly indicated trouble.

My mother jumped out of bed, followed hesitantly by my father. While my father tried to calm down the frantic neighbor, my mother proceeded to open our little store to get some medicines which she handed over to the woman.

It was late in the afternoon the next day when Lourdes came to see my mother. She thanked my mother for responding in the dead of night. She then apologized for having no money to pay for the medicines, but promised payment during harvest season in November ... ten months in the future. My mother simply told her not to forget come harvest season.

Another episode in my mother's gracious life involved Lilia, a little girl who lived with her mentally handicapped mother right across the street from our house. Lilia was seven years old when her father died. So the poor child was left to live alone with her mother. Since the mother had no source of livelihood, food came to them from time to time from the old woman's sister. Food consisted mainly of a few pounds of rice, salted fish, salted shrimp paste, a few pieces of dried meat and some vegetables. Even though the little girl never begged for food, it was apparent to my mother that Lilia was starving. Every so often she would invite her over for dinner and offer her some food to bring home to her mother. This became a daily routine until the girl grew up and became capable of taking care of herself and her mother.

In another instance, Marina, a 19 year old single mother, gave birth to a baby girl. At that time and place being a single mother was considered a disgrace to the family. Consequently, her family wanted to keep both mother and child away from the rest of the community. Needless to say the poor young mother needed help. When my mother learned about Marina's plight, she packed a few cans of milk, a feeding bottle, and some baby clothes and diapers and secretly brought these to her. My mother's "secret mission" continued for some time. Then one day my Mom brought the baby home. She took care of her for years and that baby grew up to be like a sister to me.

I remember a stranger who came to our town one stormy afternoon. The monsoon rain was pouring like hell. The wind was howling, threatening to blow away the fragile bamboo huts. He was from the city and knew no one. My mother, with my father's consent, allowed the stranger to find shelter in our home. Since he had nowhere to go, he continued to live with us and was even given a job at our little store. Gerardo turned out to be a trustworthy helper. We later found out that he lost his mother at a young age. It took several more years before we learned his deeply kept secret. It turned out that Gerardo ran away from the city because the police were looking for him after he had been implicated in a stabbing case with a drunken group of men. He claimed that my mother's good heart made him change his life.

During the early 1950s electricity was yet to be introduced into our town. Everyone used kerosene lamps during the night. My parents bought a secondhand generator to light our house and store. Since there was no doctor in our town, the only person to whom the sick could turn to for treatment was Lola Trining, our next door neighbor, who was a very accommodating and helpful nurse. The big problem was that after dusk she had only a small dimly lit kerosene lamp so she had to ask people to leave and come back in the morning. To solve the problem, my mother coaxed my father to set up an extension line for a bulb at the nurse's living room. How many lives this tender act of kindness saved, no one will ever know; but for certain we know there were many.

Being a very young child at the time when these events took place, I knew about them. However, I did not fully understand the significance of the many extraordinary things which my mother did with my father's support. But since events in childhood have a way of imprinting themselves into one's mind and heart, they have remained a part of me. And now that I have fully grasped what a  golden heart my mother had, I can not be any prouder of her. She was a symbol of a mother whose life was lived for others. Her deeds exemplified generosity, selflessness and self-giving. Charing, as she was fondly called, ... is my Mom and I am proud to be her daughter.

My father was a very young man of 23 when he married my mother at her tender age of 18. They both decided to leave La Paz, Iloilo, to start their own simple life in Dao, Antique, the town where my mother was born. The people of Dao embraced my father as their own, and when he died at the ripe old age of 86, all of the townspeople came to pay him their last respects. He was honored at the Town Hall where he served as Town Councilor for several years. Then his remains were brought to the Dao Catholic Church which was overflowing with friends and relatives. The attendance equaled, if not surpassed, that for my mother when she passed away 20 years earlier.

As a young father, he was a strict disciplinarian. He instilled in our minds, his oft repeated mantra: "Honesty is the best policy."

Probably because my parents realized the importance of a higher education which they themselves failed to obtain because of their youthful marriage, ... but who can blame my father for being swept off his feet by a pretty, well-polished, poised, big-hearted lady named Rosario Ledesma Cazenas? ... they drummed into our heads the need for a college degree from a prestigious university.

I will keep their memories alive for as long as I can by telling the story of the simple lives they lived ... simple but honorable and worth remembering and emulating. They gave me the best inheritance parents could give: the dignity and honor of a good name.

The journey which started with them still continues.

Rosario and Criste Jara
My Mother and Father

# THE FORK ON HIGHWAY 1989

Traveling in time over the uncharted Highway 1989, I came upon a three-forked intersection. Each road ahead, though completely different from each other, was equally full of promise. Which fork to take? Which road to follow? What lies ahead? A decision had to be made quickly. It was not a place where you could safely pull over and blink your hazard lights to take your time to contemplate and weigh the different options. It was even unacceptable to slow down and mull over the various possibilities lest you be hit by other oncoming vehicles whose drivers may be as confused or more confused than you are. A decision had to be made and you had to keep moving on.

It was the summer of 1989.

If I zoomed straight ahead towards the north, cruising on the same road which I have been traveling on for as long as I can remember, there were no visible obstacles. But for a few faintly discernible bumps, the path was paved and easy to drive on. To the east was another well-paved road, tree-lined and strewn with multi-colored blooming wild flowers beside it. It looked so inviting and so full of promise. I tended to go that way. To the west the highway looked forbidding. There were numerous orange cones; a clear indication of bumps, potholes, unpaved portions ... or perhaps a widening construction project ahead. I could sense that it was a risky path. Nonetheless, I felt compelled to take it.

Yoly Brondial, a former student of mine who became a teaching colleague, has moved on to become a department head at the college of engineering at De la Salle University, another highly prestigious educational institution in Manila. She has called me numerous times to offer a teaching position for approximately half my present working hours at almost twice my salary. The offer was irresistible.

Meanwhile ...

Through the years, Edith Plecis and I have been consistently communicating with each other. She has strongly encouraged me to come to the United States and to "try my luck". She herself has been teaching mathematics, our common language. "Math will take you places here. I will help you. All you need to do is come."

It was easier said than done. Leaving my family behind was the first set of orange cones to be dealt with. Although not one of them directly stood in the way, it was not easy to wave a hand and say 'So long!'. I struggled with the thought of leaving. My two elder daughters have just graduated from college. Rosanne was an engineer; Marissa was a nurse. Fine! But there were four younger children: Araceli, a nursing student; Jairus, another nursing student; Aurelius in high school, and Josel in first grade. We all had mixed emotions. They all wanted me to go ... yet, at the same time, they all wanted me to stay. So did my husband and I.

One huge orange cone was Josel. My baby was barely seven years old ... too young to fully understand the enormous changes that were about to happen. One day, I took him aside. "Josel, Mama is leaving for the States soon. Your Papa, your siblings and your Mommy (my older sister Elvie) will be with you. Is it okay with you if I go?"

"Okay, Mama."

I hugged my baby tightly and kissed him.

Then he tugged at my sleeve, "Mama, could you please buy several cans of peaches for me before you go?" Canned peaches were his favorite dessert. Back then it was a luxury in my homeland.

"Sure, I will."

And I sure did! Six large cans of peaches became my peace offering to my baby who did not realize how far away I was going.

Through all these heart-rending days, I suppressed all my emotions. I was kept busy putting everything in order. The numerous major household responsibilities I divided among my husband, my eldest daughter and my sister; the minor ones I distributed among Araceli, Jairus and Aurelius. My most precious mathematics review notes, I bequeathed to Butch Carbonell; the care of the math workbooks, to Fe Tabamo; the continuous publication of the Electronics and Communications Engineering Review Manual, to Dr. Arsol Reyes; and all other school documents, to Melvyn Alamis.

I did all of the above in secret. The truth of the matter was that uncertainty kept gnawing at me. I was dithering about leaving or staying. I was scared of the possibility of losing all my life's savings to finance the trip. I was fearful of possible failure ... failure in my quest for a better life for my family and I; failure in giving my family the opportunity to follow me sooner than later. I was in this frame of a confused mind when Edith's letter came.

*Dear Evelyn,*

*I received your last letter. I am very pleased that you are giving serious consideration to joining me here. You asked me if there is a risk involved, especially that you are coming without a work placement. Yes, there is a risk. But if you don't take risks you'll never know what you're capable of becoming.*

*So, take the risk! Come. I am here to help you in every way I can.*

*Call me as soon as you make your final decision. Either you come now or wait for another year. That would be too long a wait.*

*See you soon.*

*With warmest regards,*

*Edith*

That sealed it. I took the forbidding road to the West.
Almost a quarter of a century later, I sure am supremely glad that I did.

Lesson learned: *"Risk-taking is part of life's journey in living life to the fullest!"*

# A MEMORABLE SUPER SECRET MISSION

My wandering feet have been on a mission since I was a child. It was a summer of the late forties. School had just ended in my second grade ... or was it my third? In the little town where I grew up, the only difference between summer and the rest of the year was that schools were closed for the scorching hot months. There was not much to look forward to. It has always been that way, and having been used to it being that way, we didn't miss much. Life then was that simple. That was it, hence it was thus.

One early morning my mother's cousin came to call. Nothing unusual. She often drops by our house. What I noticed as out of the ordinary was that my mother, my Aunty Chit (my mom's older sister), and Aunt Carmelita were huddled together, speaking in whispers.

"Old people stuff," I thought to myself. I went out to play with my friend and classmate, Violeta.

Then I heard Mom. She was calling me. There was urgency in her voice. That, too, was unusual. She always left me alone when I played with Violeta.

"Belen (that was my childhood nickname), would you like to go to Manila with your Aunt Carmelita?"

My eyes lit up. "Manila! Why, of course!" Going to Manila from my rural town was like visiting New York City from a small village in Ohio.

I had been to Manila when I was five. That was not too long ago. I definitely loved to travel back to the city again.

And so ... a week later the passenger ship we boarded in Iloilo docked at the harbor in Manila. Two days later we visited an all-girls college run by nuns. I can no longer remember the details. But what I do remember was that Aunt Carmelita conferred with a gentle round-faced elderly nun, perhaps the Mother Superior, behind closed doors. Meanwhile I kept myself busy watching with delight the nuns who were going through their daily chores. They were dressed in their pre-Vatican II black habits accentuated by a white headdress that covers the neck, over which a black mantle covers the shoulders and flows down to the floor. With the exception of their faces and hands, everything was covered. I thought they looked like penguins which I had seen in a book.

After they emerged from the private conference, the Mother Superior smiled at me and said, "So my dear, I learned that you are your aunt's chaperone. How sweet of you. Are you enjoying your vacation?"

I simply nodded my head and smiled back at her.

There were several more of those visits during our two weeks stay in Manila. I was too young to ask about "old people's business". I was just enjoying the big city.

Two weeks passed. We boarded another ship. This would take us to Cebu, a city south of Manila. This trip turned out to be a very unusual one. We were the only passengers on a cargo ship. How this happened, I will never know. I never asked. I simply went along.

The ship's captain was as hospitable as a host could be. I was impressed by his clean cut looks and his crisp white uniform bedecked with stripes and some medals. He welcomed us warmly and gave us a tour of the ship calling our attention to ... "be extra careful. Watch your step!" Ropes bigger than my arms were rolled like dead snakes on the floor. At a safe distance from us, super-sized containers swung in the air as they were lifted by powerful cranes from the dock to the ship's hull.

Our sleeping quarters were adjacent to the bridge. "So you will have company all the time," was the Captain's way of explaining the location.

During our waking hours we stayed in the safety of the navigation cabin where we watched the ocean waves being sliced by the sharp tip of the ship's bow.

Before disembarking in Cebu, we thanked the captain and his crew for their hospitality.

From there, I think we took a ferry to Leyte, an island south of Cebu. We arrived in the college community of Baybay, Leyte where Aunt Carmelita's father's only sister and her family lived. She was a teacher in that college.

The atmosphere was completely different. It was neither

downright rural nor was it citified ... just a comfortably clean, quiet, self-sufficient college town with very few people. It was summer vacation. School was closed; hence there were no students around. We loved our two weeks stay there.

We boarded another ship. This brought us to still another island. Negros is south of Leyte. After an hour ferry boat ride to Iloilo, my mother and father were both on hand to drive us back home.

Ohhhhh! How I loved those travels!

By the end of that summer Aunt Carmelita bade us goodbye. She was going back to Manila to teach in that school which we recently visited.

Two years went by rapidly. We received a letter from my dear aunt that she was going to enter the convent as a postulant so as to become a nun. She also told me that during the long vacation we had together she was really secretly making arrangements for this monumental step in her life. She had to keep it a secret because of the vehement objection from her parents.

Ten ... twenty years flew by. Aunt Carmelita became not only a nun but an architect, and eventually the Mother Superior of the Congregation of the Religious of the Virgin Mary (RVM) in Quezon City, Philippines.

I felt so honored and privileged to have traveled on a top secret mission with such a devoutly religious relative during my youth.

Lesson learned: *"You never know where your little steps will lead to."*

29

# THE INVISIBLE EXISTS TOO!

I was in Cebu City, Philippines traveling with two other authors and three sales representatives from the National Bookstore, a publishing company and book store. We were on a promotional tour of a newly published series of mathematics books which I co-authored with Butch Carbonell and Jolet Felipe, as well as new publications by the other authors traveling with us.

After checking in at our hotel, we were instructed to meet in the lobby after half an hour.

My room was on the second floor. I noticed that at the end of the hallway there was a balcony overlooking the lobby.

Before going down I thought of checking out first whether the group has already gathered below. I walked over to the balcony, held on to the circular balustrade and craned forward to look down below.

Wham! Ouch! Aray! My head hit the thick floor to ceiling glass pane. It was so clean and so transparent that I did not see that it was there.

That became one of the big jokes for the rest of our trip. For each glass door that we approached someone would yell out: "Evelyn, watch out! There's glass!"


Lesson learned:  *"What you don't see is not necessarily not there."*

# THE ROCKS WITHIN MY FORTRESS

"What on earth is this heap of rocks and stones doing here?" A shocked visitor's voice coming in through my front door is audible up to my kitchen.

Right beside the door of my home, to my left as I enter, is a shelf containing piles of rocks and stones, each properly labeled and dated. They stand sentinel over my fortress, welcoming everyone to my home and inviting them to come, travel with me.

Rocks, stones ... ordinary as ordinary can be ... crude ... raw ... I picked them up from dirt roads, by the wayside, on street curbs, on the beach, by the lake, by the ocean, by the river; from the frozen glacier topped mountains to the smoldering burnt desert; within ruins of what were once-upon-a-time palaces, cathedrals, castles, fortresses; from lands which are holy as in Bethlehem to places where tragedy struck as in Tiananmen; from places of saints as in the spot of turmoil where St. Jeanne of Arc was burned; to the quiet monastery of St. Margaret of Hungary; from the architectural marvels of the Incas to the engineering masterpieces of the Aztecs ... I have collected them.

No price tags can be found on any of these precious stones. Nor are there any manufacturer's stamps. Their true worth is not answerable by "How much?", but by "Where are these from?" They are there to remind me of where I have been. They keep the memories of my wanderings alive.

I can't remember how and when I started, or how I even thought of collecting them. What I do know now, after my recent pilgrimage to the shrine of St. Therese of Lisieux in France, is that there is somebody who has preceded me in this stone collecting hobby. (See "Story of a Soul", the autobiography of St. Therese of Lisieux, 3rd Edition, Chapter VI.) I am overwhelmed to learn about this coincidence. Now I am certain that I am in the best of company!

Lesson learned: *"Priceless is defined by what may be worthless to others but precious to me."*

# A JOURNEY INTO THE HEART OF A BITTERMELON

Bittermelon. In my Filipino language we call it ampalaya.

Rarely, if ever, can one find this vegetable / fruit on the shelves of the huge grocery chain stores. I bought mine from an Asian store. My Asian palate craved for it.

Bitter? ... Yes, the leaves and the fruit are both bitter ... deliciously bitter.

Melon? Why on earth is it called a melon?

Some questions just had to be asked. I didn't really expect an answer.

The green fruit comes in various lengths, from two to twelve inches. Its circular cross section could vary from one to four inches on the biggest part. It has a smooth satin-like skin on which are engraved wavy grooves of varying depths, running lengthwise from tip to tip. Its unique look has been delicately sculpted by nature. Maturity changes it from green to golden yellow.

My bittermelon looked yellow that day. I sliced it open, revealing about a dozen mature red seeds within its bosom. "This is the beginning of a cycle of life," I muttered to myself.

Carefully, I took the seeds out of the "casing", laid them on sheets of paper towels and sat the bunch on a window sill to dry. Soon the red seeds were transformed to brown ... perhaps a foretoken of its becoming one with the brown earth in which it will find rebirth.

That was last winter.

Spring and its magic came. A clay pot came in handy. Filled with the brown earth which I dug from one corner of what will be my garden plot, I laid the seeds to rest underneath an inch of soil. A cup of cold water smoothened the microcosm of the earth's surface trapped in that tiny clay pot. I knew that underneath the handful of earth, within that small seemingly lifeless seed, was life longing to be.

There was an urge for me to say goodbye ... and yet something pulled me back from saying it. Even as the sadness of a death-like ritual filled my thoughts, the promise of a new life kept my hopes high.

Time had to do her job. But not without Mother Nature's life-giving breath. Air ... water ... sunlight ... soil ... God's blessing ... human hands to do the planting ... all these have a distinct role to play. None can be without the others.

I waited.

My garden plot hummed with the interconnectedness, interdependence and co-existence in nature.

Two weeks, ... or was it three? I have lost count. The days fly when you stop watching. There was a tiny break in the soil ... like something is pushing it up. The reality of the promise of a new life is on its way.

The mystery of the transformation from death to life unfolded. The magical beauty of a wisp of a dainty fragile green leaf popped out of the brown seed to quietly burst forth a new life. Kissed by the warmth of the sun, cooled by the gentle waft of the breeze and drenched by the sweet taste of the rain, more leaves appeared. The once tiny leaf, now full-grown, proudly displayed its delicate curly features.

Soon the seedling seemed to outgrow the confining clay pot. I could sense it begging me to transplant her to the garden plot where it could have the freedom to be. I heard her voice and heeded it.

One lovely day, just before dusk, I transplanted the bittermelon seedling to my garden plot. Now she has been freed of the clay pot's restrictions and constraints. The welcoming earth took her in its embrace. Here, anchored on the good earth, sipping the water I poured over it, she waited for the night to turn into a new day that would bring forth the light and warmth of the sun.

Days went by. Fine, fragile-looking but strong tendrils emerged among the cascades of leaves. These curly tendrils grasped and held on to something sturdier than themselves. The trellis which I have skillfully erected beside the plant was made of nothing more but a few branches and twigs from a bigger tree. Yet it became, to this plant, the sturdy friend standing by, offering its arms for the tendrils to hold on to and lending its strength for the growing plant to twist and turn its vines. From these vines emerged lovely little yellow blossoms.

Then the bees came to flirt with the flowers. And soon a little green fruit sprouted out from the base of the flower. It grew and grew and grew. Harvest time arrived. Served on the dinner table, the bittermelon fulfilled the purpose for which it existed.

Today, in the heat of summer, I plucked a golden yellow ripe fruit; one that I specially nurtured to ripen on the vine. I sliced it open. My granddaughter, Kiara, watched as the dozen or so red seeds revealed themselves.

"This, my dear child, is the beginning of another generation."

Lesson learned: *"With God's blessings we continue to journey through the cycle of life."*

# A SENTIMENTAL JOURNEY

Rev. Cornelius Hulsbosch with the Author

My sister Elena, my friend Connie, and I, with Leo as our tour planner, guide and driver, decided to make a sentimental journey to Osterbeek in the Netherlands. That was 1995.

We were to visit a retired 80 year old missionary friend who I knew since I was five years old. He has been living in a retirement house for the Mill Hill Missionaries since his retirement about fifteen years ago. Through all these years we have continuously communicated with each other through letters and cards.

Father Cornelius Hulsbosch, MHM, was one of the Dutch Catholic Missionaries who came to my hometown bringing the gifts of faith, hope and charity through the Catholic Church ... gifts for which I am profoundly grateful. To my siblings Elena, Elvira, Joeden and me, he was like a dear uncle because he and our mother shared the exact same birth date. In fact, they called each other "twins".

Before our trip I was able to make arrangements with the retirement house staff. I told Anne about our date and time of arrival. I requested her to arrange that Father Hulsbosch had no other scheduled appointments on that day and that the visit would be a surprise. She readily complied with my wishes.

Elena brought with her a framed Certificate of Recognition sent by the Dao Catholic High School in appreciation of his dedicated service to the school and the community. He was the first principal of the school. He was also the lyricist and the first person to sing the Dao Catholic High School Hymn. Elena was designated by the school to present the award to Father Hulsbosch.

We reached the retirement house at the appointed date and time. Anne was there waiting for us. Like little children guarding a deep secret, she led us to the visitors lounge where she advised us to wait while she fetched Father from his room.

Soon enough Father Hulsbosch walked into the room expecting, perhaps, one of his local visitors.

He was visibly pleasantly shocked, stunned and speechless to see us. He couldn't believe that I could pull this off on him.

He looked very good for a man of his age with health issues. Back in the Philippines many years before he retired he underwent surgery which removed one of his lungs. His doctors advised him to refrain from talking much and from singing. This was tragic as he had a magnificent voice.

So, now here we are in Osterbeek ... a long, long way from the tiny rural town in the Philippines where he lived for so many years long, long ago doing exemplary missionary work. Neither distance nor time has changed our love and respect for each other.

*"Kamo guid bala diya?"* ("Are you really here?"). He has not forgotten our dialect. We spoke in that dialect. He squeezed my arm and that of Elena's to prove to himself that we were truly there in flesh and blood. Then with that deep hearty laugh that I used to hear long ago, he turned to me and said, "If I die today, it will be your fault!" He laughed heartily again. So did we.

Elena presented the certificate to him. The room was filled with muted but overwhelming joy. He, because he felt so honored by it; us, because we were instrumental in bringing the award to him.

"Your visit and this (holding high the framed certificate) have made me very happy."

He sat down on an easy chair and we started reminiscing about the good old days. Laughter filled the little room. Then in his same old funny way he brought his finger to his lips and in a hushed tone said, "Ssssshhhh! My doctor told me to keep quiet. But I can't. You're here. I must talk. See. I'm trying to catch my breath!" Indeed, he was.

Then suddenly, in his deep baritone voice, he started to sing the DCHS Hymn. Elena and I joined in.

I desperately tried to fight back the tears from falling down my cheeks.

I looked out of the window. Snow was softly falling in Oster-beek.

Goodbye was a difficult word to say, especially when you know that without really meaning it to be so, deep in your heart it truly means farewell.

Our beloved Father Cornelius Hulsbosch died two years later. Anne magnanimously sent me a copy of his obituary.

Lesson learned: *"Distance is not a matter of space or time. It is a state of mind and emotion." ... Rolando Carbonell*

# AFTER DINNER SHOCK

July 1989. I was a newbie in this great country, the USA. I was here for only about a week. Sally and Benny, a couple who were very close family friends as well as professional colleagues back home and who are now residents of Bergenfield, NJ, invited me and six other friends for a welcome dinner party and mini-reunion at their lovely all-American home. It was my first party in America.

The gathering was so lively with everyone talking, asking questions, laughing, reminiscing, and giggling over old jokes.

The food was excellent. The company was even better. After hours of merriment, it was time to go.

Sally announced, "Hey guys, come over to the kitchen. Please take some food home. There's a lot left. Take as much as you wish. There's nobody here to eat all of this food. C'mon, help yourselves."

"Who needs more bags? Aluminum foil, anyone? Please take all the food with you." Sally sounded like she was begging us to take all that was there on the table.

I had just arrived from a third world country where food was always scarce and insufficient. Although I lived in the city all of my adult life, nothing prepared me for this.

In the midst of all the packing and bagging ... the crackling sound of the aluminum foil being wrapped around plastic plates laden with food, ... the sound of plastic bags being swiftly snapped open in the air ready to contain the plates ... the incessant cackle of endless chatter ... I stood transfixed.

"Are you okay?" Sally's voice and gentle tap on my shoulder brought me back to the reality of watching my friends pack up loads of left-overs.

"I am shocked!"

"Shocked about what?" It was Benny asking me.

"About this ... this," as I pointed to the packing frenzy taking place around the kitchen table. "You see, back home the conversation around the dinner table goes this way: 'Jairus, (Jairus is my oldest son who really loves to eat.) please don't eat all of the food. Your sister hasn't had dinner yet. She will be late because of her class schedule.' "

Then after dinner it goes this way: "Do we have anything left for tomorrow? Or is the fridge empty again?"

"But here you are practically giving away this much food. There is more than enough left over to feed fifty people. I am stunned!!!"

Then from the living room I heard Benny's voice, "Evelyn, welcome to the land of plenty and of opportunity. Welcome to America!"

Lesson learned: *"America the beautiful! America the bountiful! Thank you for sharing your beauty and bounty with the immigrant and the poor!"*

# GIANT PIZZA AND COKE

Summer 1989. It was my first day in the United States. My Filipino friends who had preceded me to the U.S.A. anticipated my arrival. They picked me up within an hour after I brought my luggage to my cousin's home. For a quick introduction to Los Angeles, they drove me around the business center.

Being a newcomer in an ultra modern American city, I was amazed at its grandiosity. I was no longer looking at magazine pictures or television screens. I had arrived!

Noontime. Hunger set in.

"Do you mind pizza and coke for lunch?"

"No, not at all. Let's go for it!"

My friends ordered pizza, ... one slice each ... and one small coke.

The orders came. I couldn't believe my eyes. The slice of pizza was like three times as big as a slice back home. The small order of coke, to me, wasn't small at all.

Thus was I introduced to the big life in America!

Lesson learned: *"Things come big here in America."*

# TRAVELING IN SIMPLE STYLE

The year was 1992. Destinations: Utah, Wyoming and South Dakota. Our purpose was to immerse ourselves in the beauty of parts of the magnificent Mountain States. Our small group was comprised of relatively new immigrants to this country, eking out a living for ourselves and sending most of our hard earned money to our families left in our native land. Leo was the tour "organizer"; Elena, Carrie and I were the "organized". All of us wanted to travel so far for so little.

This was long before the dreadful event of 9/11, 2001. There were no airport scanners at that time. Travelers came and went as freely as they wanted to. Luggage contents were not restricted nor intruded into by either human or electronic inspectors. That was freedom at its best.

Knowing that one of the biggest expenses in a tour was food, we invented our very own traveling style. We took with us a specially designated suitcase which contained a small electric rice cooker, an equally tiny electric skillet, a kitchen knife, a cooking spoon, spoons and forks (no, not plastic) and a bundle of paper towels, napkins and plates. Food was also packed in. We had rice, sausages, corned beef, spam, some not-so-perishable fruits, cookies and bread. A special recipe of pork and chicken called "adobo" was precooked and packed in aluminum foil. This entree always goes a long way without getting spoiled.

There was even one trip when we were foolish enough to also pack a gallon of water. Needless to say, the plastic container burst on the plane. At the baggage claim area, we pulled out a suitcase that was not only soaking wet, but dripping profusely!

After the flight from New Jersey, we rented a car for our driving tour, bought a disposable cooler, a bunch of water bottles and cans of soda. We were then on our way!

There seemed to be no end to the exquisite sceneries we saw as we drove delightedly for miles on traffic-free highways and country roads. What added to the great enjoyment of the trip was that we were unencumbered by any schedule or itinerary. Whenever our natural alarm systems rang for mealtime we simply looked for a park with a picnic table or some green grassy piece of land beneath the shade of a tree, parked our car, unloaded our food, and had a fun-filled picnic meal.

At the end of the day we rested our tired bodies in inexpensive but decent inns. When morning came, while we took turns freshening up ourselves, we also took turns minding the plug-in mobile kitchen which we brought with us. Food for breakfast and for the next meal were both cooked quickly. We ate a hearty breakfast and packed our picnic meal. Then we were all set for another day of an exciting sightseeing tour.

Those were the days. We traveled, we saw, we conquered part of the American Mountain States in style: our very own simple, inelegant, inexpensive style. We had so much fun for so little.

Lesson learned: *"The simple life is good and rewarding."*

# THE RED CADILLAC: SPEEDING?

Leo's picture taken from inside our red Cadillac

The year was 1993. My friends Leo and Connie, my son Jairus and I decided to take the long drive from New Jersey to Ada, Ohio to visit a friend at Ohio Northern University. It was a reunion with my childhood pen-pal, Chuck Steele, after we had completely lost contact with each other for about 35 years.

We picked up our rental car, a Honda. However, the clerk gave us the option to upgrade from a Honda to a Cadillac. The price difference was minimal so, just for the fun of it, we decided to take the brand new red Cadillac.

The drive was smooth and comfortable. In fact it was boring and uneventful ... until we were within a few miles of our destination. Leo was proceeding on a traffic-free country road. There was no other car in sight. We were all eyes on the road for signs to Ada. Suddenly, from out of nowhere, a police car started to follow us with blinking lights.

We stopped. Two officers approached us and told Leo that he was speeding. Leo handed over to one of the officers his driver's license. We were waiting for them to write a ticket. Instead they asked Leo to get out of the car. They led him to their car and had him seated inside at the passenger side. We could see what was happening through our rear window. He was being interviewed. After about a quarter of an hour, the officers let Leo out. He came back to our car. He told us that he got a ticket for speeding.

"Speeding? What speeding?" we all exclaimed.

"And that's not all," Leo said. "They asked me a lot of questions such as: Where are you going? Where do you work? Whose car is this? Who are you with? Where does each of your companions work? Where are you exactly going? Who are you visiting? How is he related to you? Why are you seeing him?"

In our naivete, we were amused by the experience. But when we explained to our host why we were delayed, he was offended by what he heard. He thought that what was done to us was wrong. We were probably stopped because we had an overly conspicuously expensive car driven by a conspicuously Asian group of people.

During those years the expression "racial profiling" was not as commonly used as it is today. Looking back, we most likely were victims of racial profiling.

Our ignorance then made light of what would have been a politically incorrect experience at present.

Lesson learned: *"Forewarned is forearmed."*

# POTS, PANS, AND A RED CADILLAC

Let us go back to the red cadillac.

Before we departed from our home state of New Jersey we were informed that one of the highlights of our trip to Ohio would be a backyard cookout. We chose to bring with us the necessary ingredients for *pancit,* a typical Filipino dish made of rice noodles, vegetables, and meat. We prepared all the ingredients in New Jersey so that they would be ready to be cooked upon arrival.

The cookout was fun and the *pancit* received center stage.

During our trip home we encountered heavy traffic as we approached the Newark International Airport where we were to return the rented Cadillac by 6:00 p.m. to avoid a rental penalty.

Since we arrived two minutes before 6:00 p.m., we unloaded our luggage in front of the rental agency office as we had insufficient time to park alongside our personal vehicle. My son Jairus, who was driving the Cadillac, jumped out of the car and ran straight to the counter to surrender the key and documents.

Still panting, Jairus exclaimed to the receiving clerk, "Whew, that was a photo finish!"

"You didn't have to rush; half an hour or so late wouldn't be a big deal," the clerk explained.

The problem was we did not know that there was some leeway for a little lateness.

Meanwhile, Connie, Leo and I were busy emptying the Cadillac trunk of our precious belongings. Out flew the brown paper bags! Out flew the pots and pans from a couple of torn paper bags. Out flew the chopping board! Out flew stuff which didn't seem to belong to such a gorgeous and expensive car. All were scattered on the sidewalk as we waited for our personal car to pick us up.

The objects coming out of the brand new shiny red Cadillac were embarrassingly inappropriate.

Lesson learned:  *"Some rules do have loopholes."*

"We live in a wonderful world that is full of beauty, charm and adventure. There is no end to the adventures we can have if only we seek them with our eyes open."

Jawaharlal Nehru

# THE PROFESSIONAL PHOTOGRAPHER

The Grand Teton

We were driving early in the morning from our hotel towards Yellowstone National Park in Wyoming. Far to our left we could see the majestic Grand Teton peering through the early morning clouds. As the sun continued to rise and break through the clouds, we could see more and more of the mountain tops emerging slowly. Suddenly, our driver stepped on the brakes. We were beside a tranquil, mirror-like lake which fully reflected the Grand Teton's magnificent snow-capped tops.

Excitedly, we all jumped out of the van. We surely didn't want to miss a rare "Kodak moment".

A few feet away from our rowdy group we saw a couple who, like us, also screeched to a sudden stop in order to enjoy the marvelous beauty of nature. The guy was clicking his camera as fast as he could adjust the focus of its lens.

He stopped using his camera briefly to adjust something. Bamba, my daughter, approached him and in her most musical and endearing voice she said, "Sir, may I request something of you? Can you please spare a few seconds to take a picture of our group?"

"Child, if I take a picture of you, you would need to pay me a good deal of green bucks. You can ask my wife to do it, though." Whereupon, he turned his gaze back to the Grand Teton, set his huge camera on a tripod and continued taking the Grand's photographs.

The wife, meanwhile, was so kind to take a picture of us with

Grand Teton looking down upon us and and with her mirror image looking up at us.

Back to our van we wondered why the man refused Bamba's simple request. Someone had a bright idea. "Didn't you notice the camera and accessories Mr. Teton had? He must be a professional photographer and being so, he wasn't at all willing to waste a second of his time to take pictures of people interfering with his works of art."

Lesson learned: *"Professionals don't take cheap shots!"*

❧❦

## TWO RIGHT TURNS THAT TURNED OUT WRONG

Time was when cell phones did not exist, nor were MapQuest nor GPS available. Those were also the days when Google and other search engines resided only in the imaginations of their creators. A phone number and an address were all that were needed to find a specific locale.

I visited Flint, Michigan to reconnect with a college friend with whom I lost touch for thirty-two years. I was able to locate her after months of diligent search using those thick and heavy phone books of the time.

I was happily successful in my search. She was a practicing physician in Flint, Michigan. I called her office and left a message a couple of times. She did not return my calls. My indomitable spirit persuaded me to call again. I left both my married name and my maiden name. This did the trick.

During my third attempt to connect, I heard the muffled voice of her secretary saying, "Dr. Alumit, this is the lady who has been calling you. She says she's Evelyn Jara, your schoolmate and dorm mate many years ago at the University of Santo Tomas in Manila. She wants to speak to you."

"Evelyn who did you say?" I heard her voice. Thirty-two years did not change that very familiar voice a bit. That same shrill tone is unmistakably her.

"Evelyn Jara, Doctor."

She took the phone and before long we were both giggling and screaming with joy having found each other after so long a time.

"Where in the U.S. are you?" She asked.

"I'm in New Jersey." I replied.

"Come over to Flint anytime. Just let me know ahead of time so I can adjust my schedule."


And so I was in Flint that summer.

One mid-afternoon, while she was busy answering many telephone calls from patients, I decided to take a leisurely walk on Parkside Avenue. I was lost in thought admiring the mansions and palatial residences in that exclusive enclave. The avenue came to an oval bend. I followed the bend. I made a right. I kept walking with the perception that I was on a street parallel to Parkside Avenue. After a while, I made another right. Surely, I thought I was back on the road where I came from. But the place looked very unfamiliar. I continued walking with the hope that I could find someone to ask directions from. There wasn't a shadow of any human form on the street ... except me. Just when I started to feel afraid, I saw a couple cleaning their front yard. With regained hope, I walked briskly towards them.

"Excuse me. Do you, by any chance, know Dr. Evelyn Alumit?"

Before I could explain my predicament the lady answered, "I'm sorry, but we have just purchased this house. We are new in the area and we don't know anyone yet. Do you know her address?"

"No, I don't."

"Do you have her phone number?"

"I'm very sorry but I don't have that either."

"Well," ... she shrugged her shoulders ... "I don't think we could be of much help."

I thanked her and continued walking.

It was starting to get dark. I knew I needed to do something. But what should I do?

I kept on walking. The streets were completely deserted. The expansive lawns in front of each house looked forbidding; the doors were shut, locked, perhaps. I have been praying silently. Now I was praying aloud. It was getting darker and darker. The avenue had no street lights.

I kept on praying while walking or perhaps I was walking while praying. I looked left and right, hoping that a kind soul would emerge from those locked mansions.

My heart leapt for joy! There, on the circular driveway trimmed with evergreen bushes in front of a huge ranch house, a young woman, a young man and an elderly man were busy loading packages into a car. I stopped at the curb at the edge of the wide manicured lawn. I waved at them and shouted a bit, "Sir, Ma'am, I need your help."

The elderly man heard me. "Come right in. How can I help you?"

"Thank God, you're out here. I am a guest of a resident in this area. I left her house a couple of hours ago for a walk, thinking that I could easily find my way back. But everything in this area is unfamiliar to me. I don't know where I am. Nor do I know how to get back to their home."

Having heard my story, Mr. Goldstein called his wife who invited me in. She pulled out of the phone stand a small book containing a list of residents in that elite gated community. She called my friend and told her not to worry because I was in their residence and would be back shortly.

Mr. and Mrs. Goldstein guided me out to the driveway where the young couple was wrapping up their loading job. She was their daughter and he was their son-in-law. Mr. Goldstein requested them to drive me back to Dr. Alumit's residence. For this, I was extremely grateful to all of them.

Meanwhile, Evelyn called off the search for me. Her son and daughter were about to start their respective cars to scour the area to look for me.

Lesson learned: *"When in unfamiliar places, an address and a phone number will lead you to where you want to go. Always have them with you."*

# TRAVELING CHEAP AND A LITTLE BIT SHY ABOUT IT

My good friend Leo is an avid traveler. He won't allow a long weekend to pass without going somewhere out of town. To be able to finance these trips without much of a dent in his pocket, he travels the most inexpensive way available. He stays in hostels or in small hotels or motels, and then tours the area by using public transport whenever possible.

Once, after coming back from one of his weekend jaunts he told the following story. Instead of taking the public bus, this time he decided to join a one day guided tour. The tour starts with a pickup at his hotel, a visit to several tourist areas, lunch, more tours; then at the end of the day he was to be dropped off at his hotel.

Fine! That sounded very convenient and fairly priced.

The tour bus schedule and route had him as the fifth of the ten pickup points. That gave him enough time to enjoy his breakfast. "What a great way to start an exciting day," he said to himself.

The day's tour turned out to be fast paced but very interesting and educational.

At the end of the tour, passengers were dropped off at their hotels. To call the attention of the passengers and to have them ready to get off, the driver called out the hotel's name as he approached the driveway.

"First stop: Hilton." Six passengers got off.

A few minutes later he announced, "Sheraton." Eleven people left.

"Next stop: Marriott." Four passengers got off. This was followed by "Doubletree Hotel." A couple stepped off the bus.

Then Leo's most feared announcement was made, "Motel 6."

"Oh, Lord," he thought to himself. "Why did they call me out immediately after those classy big name hotels?" He looked around to see if anyone other than him was getting off. There was no one else.

As he related his story, he said, "I felt embarrassed. Although I know I'm cheap, I felt cheaper than cheap this time. But I consoled myself by saying, 'Why should I care? I saw as much as the others did. We learned and enjoyed equally. Probably no one even cared where I stayed.'"

"You're perfectly right," I agreed.

Lesson learned: *"Traveling, whether in style or on low budget, takes you to the same places. It's your own personal experiences that matter."*

❧❧

## TRAVEL HAZARDS DUE TO HIGH TECH INANITY

It was a picturesque day in late September 2010 when all the deciduous trees in New Jersey were starting to display their multicolored foliage. For the first time in my life I will be flying with two of my grandchildren, Adam, age seven and Kiara, age eleven. Three of my children will also be on this trip: Rosanne, Araceli and Aurelius. We have been looking forward to a family reunion in Houston, Texas. Frat, my only brother Joeden's wife, has organized a triple birthday celebration for her and my two daughters. For reasons which only the stars could explain, the birthdays of these three wonderful family members fall on exactly the same date, although several years apart.

Newark Liberty International Airport was as busy as ever, but the check-in procedure went smoothly despite the recent controversy over the possible use of the full body scan.

The children were busy with their toys as we waited for the call to board.

A few minutes before boarding time the public address system sounded with its usual three-note chime and a voice announced, "Attention passengers of Delta Flight number 4063 bound for Memphis: there will be a slight delay in our flight. We apologize for the delay. Thank you for your patience."

Thirty minutes passed ... forty-five minutes ... one hour ... . There was no call to board. We waited patiently. One and a half hours ... still there was no announcement.

Two hours. ... Then a few more minutes later we heard the most-awaited chimes. "Passengers of flight 4063 bound for

Memphis, we are now ready to board." That was music to our ears. We had to wake the children up. Despite their excitement to fly, they had fallen asleep during the long wait.

Two hours late in leaving clearly means two hours late on arriving. We knew that we would not be able to catch our connecting flight from Memphis to Houston. The desk personnel at Newark assured us that the airline has made arrangements for our overnight stay in Memphis and that we would be booked for the earliest flight to Houston the following morning. Sounds good ... but not really ... absolutely not good if we factor in the irretrievable time lost. Immediately upon arrival in Memphis, passengers from our flight scrambled to the Delta operations desk. Aurelius and Rosanne joined the queue while the rest of us waited. The lady at the desk was fingering her allegedly all-knowing computer frantically. The line was long. She went over the flight schedule for tomorrow morning and handed over the tickets. She gave instructions where to catch the shuttle bus for the hotel. Then she handed Rosanne six vouchers of $6.00 each for dinner, another six vouchers of $6.00 each for breakfast and a sheet of paper for the hotel accommodations.

"Fine! Fine! Let's go!," we chorused.

Ten of us boarded the shuttle to the hotel; a man traveling alone, a couple and their six-month old baby, and the six of us. It was the baby's mother who started the conversation. "Did you guys look at what they gave us? They're penny-pinching us on meals. ... What decent dinner can we have for six dollars? ... But they're so stupid that they assigned three hotel rooms for us. Do they really expect my six-month old baby to have one room for herself?"

At this point Rosanne inspected our own vouchers. True enough we got the same food vouchers as the lady mentioned and six rooms booked for us! So our little boy Adam had his own room and our young girl Kiara had her own room, in addition to the four adults with their individual rooms.

Isn't that inane? Blame it on the inanimate computer which spit out the paperwork? Think again. Sometime in the not-too-distant past there must have been an "intelligent" human being called the programmer who ordered the computer what to do.

Lesson learned: *"If you think computers are infallible, think again."*

❧❧

## WATER HAS OTHER NAMES TOO

I often call myself a bundok.  This is a Filipino word which literally means mountain but which is loosely translated as a simple unsophisticated person.

One cold February evening my friend Norm, a German-American lawyer who despite his professional successes, lives a very simple life, invited me to have dinner with his friends whom I will call Mr. and Mrs. Summit.

Norm classifies himself as a bundok, too, despite the fact that he was born and lived all his life in the "mountains" of Newark, Irvington and Millburn, New Jersey, in that order.

I will be meeting Mr. and Mrs. Summit for the first time.  I have met and dined with several of his other colleagues before, including a retired judge and his wife at their country club.  For some reason, I was not at ease with what to expect this time.  Norm told me that dinner will be at an unpretentious restaurant in Summit, New Jersey.  He also suggested that I wear casual clothes, which I did.

We were to meet the couple at a designated place and time. We were on time.  A few minutes later a couple emerged from their car.  She was sophisticated in her mink coat and glittering jewelry.  He was ... well ... nothing special with his black winter coat which looked like Norm's.  But me, I was in a blue bubble jacket, dressed for a meal at McDonald's.

The restaurant wasn't really fabulous but it was set for fine dining.  Asked for drinks, they ordered some foreign-sounding wine.  Norm ordered root beer.  I ordered the safest: water.

The waiter left to get our drinks. Before he could go far, Mr. Summit called him back. "Please give us a big bottle of Evian, too."

The orders came except for my water. The couple asked if it's okay with me to share the bottle of Evian with them. I naively declined, thanked them for the offer and said, "I just want water." Little did I know that Evian was a brand name for H2O. I thought it was some exotic wine from France.

Now I know. Next time I'll order Fiji. That's water, too.


Lesson learned: *"Get to know who and WHAT you'll meet before you meet them."*


❧ ❧

## WHERE IS THE PARK?

There is no end to either or both the big and small surprises that come along your way as you explore and discover new vistas.

It was a cloudy early autumn weekend morning in 1990. The clouds didn't bother us at all and did not deter us from going on with our plans for the day. We simply hoped it would clear up as the day progressed. Nevertheless, we were ready for the rain with our umbrellas in the trunk of Leo's car.

Leo, Connie and I were pouring over the map of upstate New York. We were preparing for our game of the day which consisted of one of us closing his or her eyes then pointing to a spot on the map. The rule was for the destination to be within a two to three hours drive from where we lived in New Jersey.

Connie closed her eyes, spun around and pointed on the map. "Okay, here we go!" She opened her eyes. "Hyde Park, that's our port of call for today."

"Hide Park? Do you mean ... like we can hide in the park?"

"That's Hyde with a 'y'; not Hide with an 'i'." Leo yelled at my feigned stupidity.

"The picnic basket's ready. Let's go! Stop bickering and keep going!" That was Connie unable to hide her impatience.

Off we drove towards the Garden State Parkway. We had 90 miles to drive northward to the beautiful Hudson Valley area. The Parkway was free of traffic. That was a good sign. We crossed the state line onto the New York State Thruway, watching out for the exit towards US-9N. The map showed dots along this highway. Great! That means we are on a scenic route. Scenic, it was, indeed!

On US-9N we had to exit at Poughkeepsie. I was intrigued by the name. "Paw ... keep ... see? Whose paws are there to keep after we see them in Paw ... keep ... see?"

"Will you stop those lame jokes ... please? My grandfather told me that lame jokes cause thunder and lightning." Leo was desperately trying to be nice. What he really wanted to tell me was: "Will you just shut up!"

The peculiar name beckoned us to make a tour of the city. We saw Marist College and its impressive campus. We stopped to take a few snapshots.

Hyde Park was a few minutes drive further away. It was time for lunch when we arrived. We started looking for the park. We found none. Instead we saw a local inn. We stopped. Connie approached the lady at the desk to inquire. "Miss, where is the park in Hyde Park?

With a bemused smile, the lady answered, "Ma'am, there is no park in Hyde Park. That is just the name of this town."

"There's no park ... in ... Hyde ... Park?" Connie sounded perplexed and disappointed. So were we.

"However, you might be interested to visit President Franklin Delano Roosevelt's estate where his mansion and library are located. Then, you might also want to visit the Vanderbilt Mansion." The young lady not only succeeded in soothing our disappointment but also in arousing our interest. We asked her for specific directions. With spirited readiness she pulled out a local map from among the numerous brochures on her desk and directed us, first to the FDR museum, then to the Vanderbilt mansion.

The young lady's suggestion turned out to be a splendid idea. The picnic table near the FDR estate parking lot was what we needed most at that time. We were starving. Lunch was our utmost concern. Our picnic basket had everything we needed.

Having had our fill, we toured the presidential mansion, visited their graves, admired their garden and browsed through the exhibits in the library and museum.

A few miles from this historic site we saw the elegant Vanderbilt mansion standing majestically on an idyllic 211-acre lot situated on the east bank of the Hudson River. The well-trimmed grounds, formal gardens and natural woodlands typified the lifestyles of the wealthy American tycoons who built the railroads during the not too distant past.

We may not have found a park in Hyde Park, but we gained more than what we bargained for. Park or no park, Hyde Park is a beautiful town to visit.

Lesson learned: *"Embrace the surprises which unfold as you journey through uncharted paths."*

# BEAUTY IS IN THE EYE OF THE BEHOLDER

Vermont is a state which I wouldn't mind returning to in autumn. So when my brother-in-law Fred and his wife Becky called me up to tell me that they would want to travel to Vermont to experience the beautiful colors of fall, we immediately made plans for the trip. Fred and Becky flew in to New Jersey from the hot deserts of Arizona on a Friday afternoon.

Very early the next morning, long before sunrise, we left our home in two cars. Fred drove one car with Becky, Jose and Aurelius as passengers; Racquel drove the second car with Jairus, Bamba, and me.

Because it was still dark, we couldn't see the colors of fall along the New York Thruway. But as we drew closer and closer to Vermont, the early sunrise gave us a faint view of the colors. As soon as we crossed the state line into Vermont, the sun was up. I was most disappointed with the pale, almost anemic and lifeless, colors of the foliage. Racquel, Bamba, and Jairus were also dismayed at what they saw. They, too, had been here before.

Our walkie-talkie beeped. It was Fred asking us to pull over. They wanted to stop to take some pictures. I warned my companions from saying anything negative about the colors.

Fred jumped out of the car. Becky was right behind him. "Oh, my God," they both exclaimed. "This is so beautiful. Wow, what colors! I can't believe how gorgeous it is up here! It's awesome!" Then Becky shouted, "Only the Creator could have painted this!"

They were both extremely excited and pleased. We pretended to join them in their exhilaration.

Lesson learned: *"Truly, beauty is in the eye of the beholder."*

# ABBREVIATIONS ON THE PHONE ON THE JOB

The analytical instrument I work with in the laboratory wasn't performing as well as it should. So I called the service company. "Hello, good morning. This is Evelyn from GS Labs. I am calling for service of my instrument with serial number 34679." This is the typical opening statement for such a call.

"What specific service do you need, Evelyn?"

"The annual maintenance check."

"You need the p.m., right?"

"No, I don't need it this p.m. He may come tomorrow, a.m."

"But you called for p.m."

"I'm calling to schedule a maintenance check."

"Yes, that's p.m."

"No, not this p.m. It's almost five now and I have to leave."

"The Engineer will be there tomorrow to perform the preventive maintenance on your instrument."

"Right, so that's tomorrow a.m."

"Tomorrow a.m., you get the p.m. or the preventive maintenance service."

"Okay. Thanks." Only then did I understand that the 'p.m.' she was referring to was not the 'p.m.' that I was referring to.

Lesson Learned: *"Abbreviations lengthen and confuse conversations."*

# THE CHOOSY BEGGAR

Like most parishes in the country, the parish where I formerly worked on weekends had its church attendance diminishing; hence, its financial assets shrinking. This was happening to some parishes despite the rosy economic times of the mid 1990s.

Even so, it was not unusual to hear a knock at the door followed by a request for "food for the body" as one beggar always put it.

Although I have always wondered why these able bodied men didn't go out and get themselves jobs, I would ask them to wait while I prepared a couple of sandwiches in the kitchen.

One Sunday, one of my weekly visitors came as expected. I was about to start our ritual-like "wait-while-I-prepare-some-for-you" routine, when he stopped me in my tracks with a loud voice, "Miss, what are you going to prepare for me?"

"Peanut butter sandwich." I replied as I turned towards the kitchen.

"Miss, Miss," he called out again. "Did you say peanut butter sandwich? I don't like that."

"But that's all we have in this rectory."

"Don't you have ham or turkey with lettuce and tomato?"

"Sorry, we don't have that."

With disbelief I muttered to myself, "Unbelievable! He has the nerve to be choosy."

He left without the peanut butter sandwich.

Lesson learned: *"If you think beggars can't be choosers, think again."*

61

# IF . . .

The laboratory where I work does not have any phone system dedicated for chemists and technicians who work on the bench. Although employees are asked not to use management's desk phones, exceptions are sometimes allowed when there is a grave necessity as when a member of one's immediate family is ill. One such exception was given to Amna who was caring for her sick sister. A public address system is used to call the attention of employees who have no phones on their desks.

One early morning we heard the not-so-often used public address system click on and Bibi, our front desk secretary, came on with a booming voice. "Amna, you have a call on extension one."

Since it was Amna's day off, nobody took the call. A minute later Bibi was on the public address system again. "Amna, please pick up on extension one." Naturally no one picked up the phone.

Another minute of silence and Bibi was on again. "Amna, if you are here, pick up on one; if you are not here, don't!"

Lesson learned: *"Can all those who are absent please raise their hands?"*

# THE LAWYER HAD NO DOLLAR TO SPARE

The commute from the Newark Penn Station to Jersey City, both in New Jersey, takes about half an hour. Mr. Norman S. Karpf, a New Jersey certified civil trial attorney, prefers the convenience of this train ride over the hassle of driving through the traffic-laden highways and streets between the two cities. By taking the train and walking a few blocks to the Court House, he is given the opportunity to enjoy a healthy early morning walk.

Travel by train, though, is not without some disadvantages. One of these is the nuisance caused by beggars at the train stations.

One morning as Mr. Karpf hurried to catch his train, a tall muscular male beggar approached him. "Sir, do you have a dollar to spare?"

Mr. Karpf looked at the man and then without missing a beat he responded, "I don't have a dollar. But can you spare me a quarter?"

The overbearing beggar walked away with a puzzled look on his face.

Lesson learned: *"Quick of wit, quick to the draw!"*

# THE LADY OF CARMEL

The Lone Cypress

The drive from San Francisco to Los Angeles via Highway 101 brought us to one of those locations which stands out for its natural scenery. This is Carmel-by-the-Sea. The spot where the more than 200-year old "Lone Cypress" stands has a delightful beauty of its own. This probably explains why most of the early inhabitants of the area were artists, poets, writers, and later on, actors and actresses. In fact, the famous actor and director Clint Eastwood was the mayor of this town in the late 1980s.

When we visited the town in 1991, we immediately noticed something unusual. The houses were not numbered. Were they trying to conceal something from someone? Or is it because everyone knew everyone else? But how did the mailman manage to deliver the mail properly?

How did a visitor find the house he was searching for?

Our curiosity deepened so we continued driving through the streets of the city. We got engrossed in the beautiful houses and gardens. When it was time to leave, we had a serious problem. We somehow lost our bearings and couldn't seem to get out of the city. We couldn't find the entrance to the highway.

We felt hopeless as we drove around in circles. There were no pedestrians to inquire directions from. After a short while we saw an elegant lady driving her equally elegant convertible. We waved at her; she waved back at us. We slowed down; she did, too.

"Ma'am, we need your help. We have been going around for

about half an hour but we can't find the road back to the highway. Can you please give us directions?"

"You know what? It's really tough in here. I can't give you directions, but I know how to get there. Follow me!"

With that she stepped on the gas, waved her hand, and led the way!


Lesson learned: *"When lost, find the right someone to lead the way."*


ﻉﺟ ﺟﻉ


## FAST FOOD

I don't remember the month, but it must have been sometime in the late spring of 1991. Loida, Leo and myself decided to fly to Los Angeles, drive down south to Death Valley, up north to San Francisco, then back to Los Angeles.

Loida and I were first-time travelers on the West Coast. Leo has been to L.A. before but he hasn't travelled as extensively as on this visit. Then one night at about 8:00 pm, while we were driving from San Francisco to Los Angeles, the pangs of hunger hit all three of us. The unanimous decision was to get off the highway at the very next exit, look for a fast food place, pick up some food, and drive on.

Leo was driving fast for two reasons. First, we were very hungry. Second, we still had a long way to go.

At one point Loida and I suddenly hollered to Leo, "Oh my God, Leo, drive slowly! We just passed an exit."

"Calm down, calm down, girls. Don't panic. There will be a next one. Keep your eyes on the signs. Let me know when you see the next E - X - I - T."

We saw the next one. "Get off this highway. Now!"

He did. We drove around but couldn't find any fast food chain. After what seemed to be a futile attempt to locate one, we saw an elderly gentleman walking his dog. We stopped. I got out of the car. "Good evening, Sir. Can you please tell us where we can find a McDonald's?"

The gentleman eyed me curiously. "Ah, do you mean one of those fast food chains?"

Under my breath I said to myself, "What kind of ignoramus in America doesn't seem to know McDonald's?"

"Yes, Sir." I responded politely.

"Oh, we don't have any of those kinds here. This is Santa Barbara!"

"Santa Barbara! Ora pro nobis! ... Huh????" I muttered to myself as I courteously thanked the old man.

Both Leo and Loida overheard our conversation. I got back to the car, surprised and bewildered. "What is it about Santa Barbara that McDonald's seems foreign to them?" We asked each other.

We reached L. A. after getting our McDo burgers and chicken nuggets in another town. We told our friends about our Santa Barbara experience and they all made fun of our ignorance. "You see, in Santa Barbara, people are allergic to cheap fast food. They eat only in classy and pricey restaurants. Now, do you get it?"

Yes, we got it!

Lesson learned: *"Do you know where you're going to?"*

# THE HAZARDS OF A BRAND NEW CAR

We were set for a long drive from Salt Lake City, Utah to Spring Lake, Colorado and beyond. Picking up our rental car, a brand new Lincoln, was exciting. We looked forward to a very comfortable and smooth ride.

We were enjoying our ride as well as the scenery. As we crossed the state line and drove into Colorado, we were tapping to the music over the radio. The open highway, clear of all traffic, was very much unlike New York and New Jersey where we came from. It was a new unhurried experience for us.

Just as we began our Colorado experience, Leo saw the blinking lights of a Colorado State Police car right behind us. "Uh, uh, what have I done wrong?" Leo wondered. He stopped and waited for the officer to approach us.

There were five of us in the car. All were wondering why in heaven's name we seemed to be in trouble. Speeding was out of the question. Leo was driving within limits.

The officer approached the driver's side.

As Leo handed over his driver's license, he meekly greeted the officer. "Good morning, officer. What's the problem?"

The officer looked at Leo's driver's license. Noting that he was from New Jersey, he said, "From New Jersey, huh? Can I see the rental papers for this car?"

Leo handed the documents over to him. We were still wondering why we were stopped. A lot of unpleasant scenarios were playing in my head. We would be delayed. We would be ticketed. We had to go to court, etc., etc. We would be made to pay a stiff fine. Finally, I couldn't help myself but speak out, "Officer, we are tourists. It's our first time to see your beautiful state. We would very much want to enjoy our stay here. Are we in trouble, Sir?"

"Your brand new car doesn't have a plate number."

"No, Officer, it does." All of us simultaneously pointed out to him the temporary plate number displayed on the left rear window.

"Okay, so there it is. This is not properly displayed. Now, let me help you display it properly." He went back to his car, took a roll of tape and came back to us with it.

"Now, guys, take that paper out from there and display it on the rear window. Be sure that it is clearly visible. Here's the tape. Help yourselves to it."

He then handed us his business card. "If you have any problem, don't hesitate to give me a call. Welcome to Colorado. Have a safe trip and enjoy your stay in Colorado!" With that he waved us on our way.

All of us heaved a sigh of relief. We thanked him and continued on our way.

When we got back to New Jersey, I wrote the officer, commending him for his kindness.

A few weeks later I received a nice letter from his superior thanking me for the letter and informing me that the letter of commendation will be kept in his file.

Lesson learned: *"A good word for a good deed is good, indeed!"*

*"Not all those who wander are lost."*

J. R. R. Tolkien

# THE COTTAGE BY THE WAYSIDE

Fall in Vermont, I was told, is like no other. The colors are more vibrant and crisp, the red and purple are deeper, the yellow and gold are brighter, even the white is whiter especially when it accentuates the dark green of the evergreens. Then there's the rosy pink and the earthy brown, and numerous other shades in between.

With this in mind, Jairus, Connie, Leo, Elena, and I set out on a "leaf-peeping" expedition one sunny October weekend, in 1992. It was another one of our spur of the moment decisions; hence there was no pre-planned destination nor lodging. We only knew that we wanted to spend the weekend in Vermont.

Along the way we stopped at a garage sale. We love to browse through someone else's junk with the hope of finding some treasure.

This particular day Connie and I were both attracted to knives. I bought a small paring knife with a beautifully sculpted bone handle. Connie bought a big butcher knife. She loves to cook. So this would come in handy when chopping beef, pork or chicken with bones.

At about four in the afternoon we stopped at a convenience store for two reasons. We needed groceries, food and water. Leo needed a pay phone to make a reservation for hotel rooms for us. Cell phones were still unheard of at that time.

"Sorry, all our rooms are booked." This was all he got for an answer. He tried calling another hotel. He received the same answer.

"I'll try again later," he said as we headed back to our car.

"After another hour on the road we stopped at a gas station to fill up. Leo made another call to still another hotel. They, too, were fully booked. Darkness had started to cover the land around us. Still we had nowhere to sleep for the night. The manager of the gas station overheard our conversation and understood our predicament. He explained to us that during the peak of the foliage season, all hotels are booked. But he has a friend who rents out his cottage. "Would you, guys, want to give it a shot?"

"By all means, yes." We eagerly responded.

"Give me a minute. I'll give him a call. I hope it hasn't been booked yet."

We waited.

"Hello, Greg. Jerry here. How're you, buddy? I have a group of five tourists from New Jersey here at my station. They're looking for an overnight accommodation around the vicinity. Is your cottage still available?"

There was a brief silence. Evidently, Greg was saying something to Jerry.

"Okay, okay. So you want to meet them at the Pathmark parking lot. Okay. ... Oh, they would want to know how much. ... Okay ... alright. ... I'll let them know. Will you hold on a minute, please." At this instant he asked if $120.00 would be okay with us.

Between sleeping in our car and sleeping in a cottage, without much thought we preferred ... rather, grabbed ... the latter.

"Greg, they're meeting you in ten minutes." Jerry hung up the phone and turned to speak to us. "Okay, guys, about eight miles from here you will see Pathmark on your left. Drive into the parking lot. There you will find a white truck with this plate number." He handed a piece of paper on which he wrote the plate number. "Greg will keep his lights on for you to locate him easily."

We thanked Jerry for his concern and kindness and we went on our way.


Finding Greg wasn't a problem at all. Leo and Jairus jumped out of the car to speak to him.

"My cottage is about twenty minutes drive from here. I'll take you there. Just follow me."

And so, our odyssey began. Three minutes after we left the

parking lot we made a left turn from the highway to a country road. The road was deserted. There were no vehicles, no buildings nor residences, no lights, only trees on both sides. Connie was the first to panic. She wanted us to turn back. Jokingly, I reminded her, "Connie, look! Don't you remember that you have a big butcher knife in the trunk?" We all laughed. This somehow lightened the mood for a while. But as we continued to drive behind Greg's truck on that deserted road, dreadful scenarios played upon our imaginations. Nevertheless, we continued following him. Our apprehensions grew more intense when we turned left to an unpaved gravel road.

"Oh, God, what are we doing? Where is this stranger taking us?" Still we kept on following him. Five minutes ... six ... seven. We were still on the gravel road to nowhere ... so it seemed.

Then ... wow! The road brought us to a big rotunda surrounded by about ten well-lighted cottages. We parked in front of a yellow one.

"This is it, guys."

It was a lovely house in a quiet neighborhood. Now all our fears were gone. Greg pushed the door open. I couldn't help asking. "Greg, your house is not locked?"

"No, it's not. This is Vermont!"

We sat down in the cozy living room. After a short conversation, we gave him the money. He handed us a key. "If you feel safer with the lock on, you may use this. And, by the way, tomorrow, as soon as the sun is up, take that path beside the cottage. A short walk will give you considerable enjoyment. There will be a pleasant surprise for you."

Early the next morning, after our breakfast of coffee, sausages and rolls which we bought from the convenience store, we set out for a walk on the narrow path. Where the path ended, an incredible sight unfolded before us. There was a serene lake surrounded by trees which gloriously exhibited a spectacular rainbow of autumn colors. A mirror image was clearly visible in the lake. A number of little boats enhanced the already wonderful scenery.

What we went through last night was more than compensated for by this heavenly display of nature's painting splashed with all the colors only a Vermont autumn can unveil.

Lesson learned: *"Don't be afraid when life throws you a curve ball; just catch it. A rainbow could be tucked in it."*

❧❧

## THE WET FLOOD VERSUS THE DRY FLOOD

The year was 1611. That was precisely four centuries ago! My beloved Alma Mater, the Pontifical and Royal University of Santo Tomas, the Catholic University of the Philippines, more lovingly called simply "UST" which we playfully pronounce as "Oooossste", is celebrating her 400th birthday. Among its laurels are its graduates ... thousands upon thousands of professionals who have been endowed with God's blessings of the Thomasian Spirit of godliness, professionalism, dignity, honor, leadership, sense of responsibility, and the willingness to serve around the world.

These graduates have filled the four corners of the globe. With the education imparted to them by the University during their student years, they share their knowledge and expertise to make our world a better place.

A grandiose celebration has taken place in the Philippines. A great number of us who could not travel back to the motherland wanted to join in the revelry.

With this in mind, Rev. Fr. JM Manolo Punzalan, an Adjunct Priest at St. Joseph Parish in Maplewood, New Jersey, and an alumnus of the UST Seminary, organized a Quadricentennial celebration that coincided with the feast of Saint Thomas Aquinas, UST's patron saint.

January 28, 2011 was a couple of days after the big snowstorm on the East Coast. New Jersey became a white state, fully covered with snow. Where the city plows have done their job, there remained four to six feet high piles of snow. Where the residents have cleared the sidewalk, you could see a black meandering lane, one foot wide at most, which goes through, bordered by the white snow piles on both sides.

While walking through this pathway from the parking lot to the church where we had to gather for the celebration, we remembered the one experience which no student of UST could escape. The city of Manila, where the UST campus is located, is below sea level. Each year, during the rainy season, when the monsoons generously pour tons upon tons of raindrops on the city, the campus and its surrounding area get flooded, ankle-deep if you're lucky, waist-deep if you're luckier! If the rain pours during the night, students and faculty alike welcome happily the day off. But if the rains come in the middle of the day when everyone is already in school, this becomes a nightmare. To be able to get home from the campus there was no choice but to wade in the murky waters of the flooded streets. That was an inescapable part of the UST students' life.

As we carefully inched our way between piles of snow, the memories came back to life. Whereupon, Med Domingo, a fellow Thomasian commented, "The sad thing about the flood in UST is that we had to wade and get wet in it. On the other hand the good thing about the 'flood' in NJ is that we stay dry. We simply push the 'solid white water' and pile it up on both sides of the sidewalk. It obediently stays within its boundaries and we remain dry as we walk between the piles. It reminds me of the parted Red Sea."


Lesson learned: *"Even floods have two versions: one is wet and the other is dry."*

# TIME TRAVEL

Time travels at the speed of 24 hours per day, 7 days per week, 365 days per year, give or take a few seconds. Traveling at this speed for fifty years is a demanding, extensive and exhausting process. Some of us are blest to get there, reaching that golden age and able to look back and view the winding path which brought us to the present.

Like most travelers in time, I have somehow unconsciously stopped counting the years. So it was a big and pleasant surprise when in August 2009 I received an email from Dr. Bernadette Duran, Head of the Chemical Engineering Department, UST, who was one of my best students when we were decades younger. They will be celebrating the 75th Anniversary of the Chemical Engineering Department. They were preparing a Souvenir Journal for this milestone and she requested that I write an article about her department during the 1960s.

Excitedly, I traveled back in time. I vividly remembered several significant events of that decade.

Nineteen sixty! It was the beginning of another decade. It was my third year as a student of engineering; my first year as a Chemical Engineering major. During the previous two years, I had worn to school my modestly sleeved white blouse with a closed neckline topped by a shirt collar, complemented by a gray pleated skirt that fell far below the knees. This was the official female engineering students' school uniform. For the third year now I would be falling into the familiar daily routine of bearing left as soon as I entered the building, a habit ingrained in all female engineering students. The reason for this was that during that period in time segregation by gender was the norm at the University. Ladies were required to use the left side stairs; men were required to use the right side stairs. Ladies used the left side canteen; men, the right side. Ladies were enrolled in the morning section. Usually, men were enrolled in the afternoon and evening sections.

Looking back, in some respects the Chemical Engineering curriculum was different during the 1960s. The five-year course did not include Differential Equations, Chemical Kinetics nor Statistics. All engineering courses were capped by a graduation in June. While other colleges held their graduation rites right after the school year ended in April, students of the Faculty of Engineering were compelled to do "hard labor" for two sweltering summer months at the "sweat shops" of a classroom of 40 to 50 students, inadequately cooled by one ceiling fan. This "labor camp", otherwise known as the 5-unit Integration Course or Review Classes for the Engineering Board Exams, was a prerequisite for graduation. Graded examinations which were given daily culminated in a grueling 3-day final exam which was patterned after the actual government-conducted board exams. The fortunate students who passed graduated in June. The unfortunate ones had to wait one full year for a second opportunity to sit for the Integration Course. That was really, truly tough and painfully disappointing.

To their credit the B.S.Ch.E. graduates of that decade were prolific in Summa, Magna and Cum Laudes. The results of the Board Exams gave credence to their abilities. No result was ever without one or more UST graduates in the top ten! Likewise, all the members of the teaching staff were the so-called "Creme de la Creme". They graduated with high honors. The teaching position was earned by the wave of the hand of the Father Regent who always kept a close eye on those who were about to graduate with honors. On the same day that the list of graduates was released he personally called the qualified person and offered him / her a teaching position. It was a distinct honor to receive that offer.

Once you accepted the offer, you were expected to be prepared to teach any and all subjects which you were assigned. These included some "non-technical subjects", otherwise known as "cultural subjects". Thus, for instance, my Spanish teacher was a Chemical Engineer who could hardly speak a sentence of Spanish. Thus did I teach Theology and Public Speaking. ... What did I really know about these subjects? ... Somehow I survived. Only much later ... several years later ... did we, the "technical teaching staff", breathe a sigh of relief when we were finally allowed to focus on teaching only technical / science / mathematics / engineering subjects.

The members of the faculty were as one family, sharing one common faculty room whose walls were lined with tiny lockers. You were lucky to have one locker all to yourself. Usually you shared a locker with one or two more teachers. In that tiny room there was one desk for the Dean; another for the Father Regent; one for the Faculty Secretary; one corner table for the clerk who did the typing and mimeographing; and one long table for the teaching staff to share. It was not surprising that the latter was "standing room only" most of the time. And, yes, in one secluded corner was the mimeograph machine where confidential papers and test questions were printed. Paradoxically, these conditions helped bring about a wonderful camaraderie among us.

It was during this period when the "brain drain" took place. There was a mass exodus of a large number of faculty members to the U.S.A. Some left as immigrants; some as scholars; some on Assistantship programs. Most of them never returned to the Philippines. They stayed and practiced their professions in the U.S.A. with considerable success.

In 1968, the Engineering Faculty Organization was instituted. Miss Angelica Granados, B.S.Ch.E.'62, was the founding President. The entire teaching staff belonged to this organization ... a single group working together for the good of all. Yet, asking for a raise, a promotion, or for more benefits never came to mind. Our thinking was: whatever remuneration was given to us ... that was it. Our only request as an organization was for more chairs. Life was simpler then, and we had simpler needs.

But that was then ... some half a century ago ... when life was comparatively uncomplicated, needs were basic and minimal, distractions were few and far between. Much water has passed under the bridge since then. We cannot go back, but we can reflect fondly on our experiences, taking pride in the fact that what we went through then were the foundations of what we are now.

Half a century of travel is no mean feat. The world has changed so drastically; technology has made the change faster than the blink of an eye. We have traveled so far. Oddly, though, the inner person has remained almost the same.

Lesson learned: *"Despite numerous innovations during the passage of time the inner core remains essentially constant."*

# BEYOND THE VALLEY OF DEATH

Death Valley

Leo, Loida, and I had an ambitious plan for our week-long trip to California. We were to fly to Los Angeles, rent a car, then drive down to Death Valley, drive through Bakersfield, then up north to San Francisco via Sacramento, and finally back to Los Angeles after having traveled along the coast and stopping briefly at Carmel.

A brochure described Death Valley as the "Hottest, Driest, Lowest: A superlative desert of streaming sand dunes, multicolored layers of rocks, canyons and wilderness."

We were in the middle of this barren land more than 200 feet below sea level. I remembered that I have read somewhere that this arid place was once ... millions or so years ago ... the site of a succession of inland lakes, collectively known as Lake Manly.

It was an incredible feeling to be in such a unique environment. We lingered, lost in thought ... admiring such beauty of nature ... contemplating on how natural changes do occur on the earth's surface through time. What we forgot was the passage of time. Sunset came earlier and faster than we thought.

We hastily left Death Valley, frightened that we would not be out of the desert before total darkness falls.

Leo was the driver. I was the navigator. Loida was the lookout. (For what? We didn't really know.)

It was now dark and we were in an uninhabited area. We were

low on gas. The map indicated that we were approaching a fork in the road. We could not afford to make the wrong turn at the fork. Loida helped me with the map as Leo started to slow down. He thought that it would be unsafe to make a full stop. After a quick analysis of the map, we decided to take the right fork.

Except for the beams from our headlights, it was pitch black. We were approaching a mountainous region. We were driving on a zigzag road when suddenly the beam of light hit something which reflected like a human skeleton hanging somewhere ahead of us. I kept my calm but requested the two of them to join me in praying The Lord's Prayer and the Hail Mary. Although I did not tell them what I saw, we were all nervous at this point.

The wilderness seemed to be endless. An hour must have passed. We kept an eye on the map and any signs that would indicate we were going in the right direction. Then as we reached the crest of a hill I saw flickering lights at a distance. Excitedly, I called out, "Look! I think I see light!" Within a couple of minutes we lost sight of it again. Was it an illusion? Was my imagination playing a game with me?

There was no choice but to keep on driving. We found ourselves on the crest of another hill. Again we saw the lights. This time they were brighter and nearer. Spontaneously, like Columbus seeing land for the first time after months of seeing nothing but water, the three of us applauded, clapped and cheered. "Civilization is here! We have landed!"

Lesson learned: *"A flicker of light is all we need to defeat the depth of darkness."*

"Once you have traveled, the voyage never ends, but is played out over and over again in the quietest chambers. The mind can never break off from the journey."

Pat Conroy

# REFLECTIONS ON REFLECTIONS

Twenty years have passed ... flown, is perhaps the better word. The mind sometimes likes to play its games. For certain events the year 1991 seemed like it was ages ago; for others it may seem like it was a not too distant past. Today is 2011. Using my timeless mathematical tools of fingers and toes, I counted exactly twenty ... yes, that was twenty years ago ... Twenty long years? Or simply twenty short years? My mind has a confused answer.

Serendipity. That's how this happened. I was spring cleaning ... specifically dusting off the dirt which remained invisible during the winter but somehow makes itself clearly visible in spring. After two hours of going through the boring routine of wiping and rearranging, I pulled out one of my growing collection of photograph albums. The first page shouted out at me thus, "I'm twenty years old. Do you hear me? I'm twenty! Care to look back?"

Eagerly, I did.

I sat comfortably on my rocking chair, (reminiscent of President John F. Kennedy); then leafed through the pages of the now-dusty brown plastic covered album. Twenty years didn't seem that distant. I thought to myself, "If I travel through this same route today I guess I'll see the same grand and awesome places. But probably I wouldn't feel the same impact as when I saw them the first time."

The reflections I had written with steadier strokes of a more youthful hand ... a hand that was twenty years younger ... and a mind which was more easily affected by new and wondrous experiences ... brought forth a strong urge in me to reflect upon those reflections.

Upon opening the first page, on a photograph of a tree, part fallen and broken, part alive and still lush, bent over but still strong, my handwritten note reads:

> In the book of Zen, the student asked the Master: "What is the greatest of the wonders of the world?"
> "The greatest wonder," answered the Master, "is your consciousness of these wonders."

At the back of the picture is written: Carmel by the Sea.

Indeed, looking at the picture I wonder how that distorted fallen trunk, broken twice over, still rests courageously and radiates a unique beauty. Perhaps it is there to teach us a lesson: "There is gracefulness even in our brokenness; for Christ in his most broken and disfigured state exists as the strongest sign of love."

The next picture showed silhouettes of Loida and me with the bright sun-drenched Beverly Hills Hotel behind us. I stared at the picture and thought to myself, "This symbolizes the contrast between the bright and dazzling glitter of the rich and famous of the entertainment world versus the innumerable faceless humans whom the world does not see. And yet these innumerable nameless faces are the ones who make the world go round. For isn't it a fact that the world could function smoothly without movies, movie stars and the whole celluloid world? And yet think of the world without garbage collectors, the employees who work at this hotel, the farmhands and the farmers, the plumbers and the mechanics, the electricians and the engineers, the nurses aides and the nurses, the police officers, firemen, military personnel, the myriad unknowns who work without titles while manning the assembly lines in huge factories and production plants. Looking at the bigger picture of life, aren't they the indispensable people? Aren't they the faceless nameless silhouettes throughout the world?"

Another picture is captioned "*Malibu Beach and the Pacific Ocean.*" I have reached the other side of the ocean of my dreams. Indeed, I have been richly blessed by God to see beyond my own prayers and dreams. There is much wisdom to the profound human ambition ... "Reach beyond your grasp!"

On a picture taken on top of Mt. Wilson, at the Griffith Observatory, I wrote: *"It must be heavenly to see far beyond what the naked eye could see!"* I am strongly convinced it is.

From the mountain top we drove down to the UCLA campus. I posed in front of the building named School of Engineering and Applied Sciences. Underneath the picture I wrote: *"I found a connection here."* Reflecting on that succinct comment, I now look back and say, "Actually, it was a disconnection which I found. Because twenty years ago I focused upon educating would-be engineers. I left that profession to find myself in a completely different, more profound and wider world ... with no regrets."

Then down south to Las Vegas. A picture taken on the "Strip" is captioned: *"The world's most lavish and exciting resorts on the earth's most brightly-lit spot at night!"* The passage of twenty years has not made that city any older. In fact Las Vegas now looks as young as ever, more lavish and more brightly lit.

The early hours of the next morning. A picture with Lake Mead in the background is captioned; *"Oh, what a beautiful morning! Oh, what a beautiful day! The morning sun spreading its golden rays unto the mountains. Man's hand enhancing the beauty of God's work."* I still feel the same way about that. Beautiful Lake Mead is America's largest man-made reservoir. The mountains referred to line the gateway from the lake to Hoover Dam. They direct and restrict the water's path. Water flows to where it is desired and needed in accordance with the engineering design for this powerful super-structure.

On another photograph where the turbines of Hoover Dam could be seen, I have written: *"Behold the water that turns the turbines that generate the power which lights the darkness and moves the industries that shape the world! A symbol of man's genius making good use of God's creations."* Upon reflecting on what I wrote, I now have a fuller and a deeper experiential grasp of the biblical text: *"God looked at everything He had made, and He found it very good." (Genesis 1:31).* The Lake Mead - Hoover Dam engineering marvel is a classic example of man harnessing nature for productive purposes. It is with sadness that we are aware of other human endeavors which harness the good things of earth for what is counterproductive or evil.

Beneath a picture with a sign "Welcome to Arizona" I wrote, *"We have just crossed the time zone. Between Nevada and Arizona, a time difference of one hour begins here."* I remember that somewhere near this same spot were two huge clocks, one on the Arizona side and another on the Nevada side. One showed the time as 1:30 while the other indicated 2:30. There was an invisible line separating the continuous land surface into two discontinuous time frames. Even now, twenty years later, I am still searching for an explanation. I eventually learned the answer from St. Augustine who wrote, *"What then is time? If no one asks me, I know what it is. If I wish to explain it to him who asks, I do not know."*

Several pages containing stunning pictures of the awesome Grand Canyon follow. I flipped them back and forth looking for something I might have written. Much to my surprise, I have written nothing. My inevitable conclusion is that such unequaled natural beauty which is still being continuously sculpted by the mighty power of the Colorado River has made me speechless. My mind went blank. It still is.

Then on to Death Valley. *"Barren and desolate but with a unique beauty of its own,"* was the caption written beneath a picture of the landscape. Another photograph showing an open train-like horse-drawn locomotive was labeled, *"This locomotive seems to say that Father Time died here."* Now as I sit on my rocking chair, I think of what time has done to the objects on those two pictures. The landscape is definitely unchanged. Twenty years can only succeed in making a perceptible change on a landscape if there were a cataclysmic event. Thank God, there hasn't been any within the past two decades. But that locomotive. Is it still there? Maybe so. Is that handsome horse still there? Maybe not.

The next photo was taken at the edge of the desert. The caption reads, *"In the wee hours of the morning ... somewhere among the cacti of a California desert."* I remember vividly how this picture was taken. It was semi-dark. The sun was still hiding behind the wings of night. The powerful headlights of our car revealed numerous blooming cacti at the edge of the road. We stopped, jumped out of the car, left the headlights on to focus their beams on the cacti, and took a lovely picture of them.

Ahhhhh! The beauty of wildflowers! My mind rushed to the

biblical passage: *"Consider how the lilies grow. They do not labor or spin. Yet I tell you, not even Solomon in all his splendor was dressed like one of these." (Luke 12:27)* These cacti blooming in the wilderness, uncared for by human hands, fit into the same category as the lilies mentioned above.

About an hour or so later the sun had risen. We stopped for another picture beside fruit-laden trees in an orchard. The caption reads: *"... and at daybreak, where land is desert no more, oranges display their bounty and their beauty."* I picked up a Sunkist orange from the table beside my chair. Could this have come from the orchard where this picture was taken twenty years ago? I do hope so. ... Or has that area been unmercifully bulldozed to give way to the encroaching housing development projects? I truly hope not!

The next several pictures were taken in the Yosemite National Park. The first one showed us having a picnic beside a river, and the caption goes this way: ... *"Soon we realized that food for the eyes cannot replace food for the belly ..."* Even now, this truth still holds.

Then the El Capitan towers from a distance ... *"A glimpse of power, strength and serenity."* That formidable natural structure still stands to symbolize these attributes.

A stream of water washing the face of a lofty rocky mountain comes next. I reflected on the waterfall as ... *"Life cascading from the heights is love overflowing from nature's bosom."* I still feel that way ... even now.

Then The Dome. I wrote, *"The Dome looks like a temple ... a center of communication between nature and God ... from which messages of thanks are sent to God for the elegance and beauty of His world."* I would say that twenty years has not changed my thoughts about that isolated dome-like rock.

The Golden Gate Bridge. *"The orange bridge."* That caption focused on what I saw: the orange paint of the bridge. It was more of a question than a naive statement; "Why orange, not golden?". At that time my thoughts abruptly ended. Now I know better. "Golden Gate" has nothing to do with the color. It is so named because it crosses the Golden Gate Strait which is the entrance to

San Francisco Bay from the Pacific Ocean. Irving Morrow, the Golden Gate consulting architect, selected orange as it complements the natural surrounding colors and enhances the visibility of the bridge despite the frequently penetrating fog.

That is a reaction which I have outgrown over the years. It was a stupid reference to the visible, forgetting the essential meaning for which the name of the bridge stands.

At the crookedest road in San Francisco, I wrote: *"Extraordinary! Exciting! Beautiful!"*

That is still true to this day.

Lesson learned: *"Occasionally, when we look back we sense a subtle inference of growth."*

## BROWN BAG LUNCH

The journey through the ordinary daily changes in life inevitably takes you to dentists, doctors, medical laboratories, chiropractors, frequent trips to the pharmacy and other necessities of that nature. Or it could also take you to what most seniors do, like playing bingo, joining knitting groups, taking line dancing lessons, taking trips to the casino, or simply watching a classic movie at the town library.

If you want to watch the free movies shown at Springfield Library in New Jersey, it is suggested that you bring a brown bag lunch with you. "Why brown? Can it not be any other color," I asked. Later, I learned that "brown bag lunch" is an expression meaning "a simple lunch for yourself". Brown came from the fact that in the past, most of these lunches were carried in brown paper bags.

I was at one of the medical clinics recently for my biannual lab tests. Not that I haven't been to any of these clinics before. It was just that this was the first time I arrived late in the day. In the past I always saw to it that I get there before opening time to avoid the long wait.

As I entered the waiting room, it was a "standing room only" situation. The room was packed with people and most of them were holding brown paper bags. A kind lady instructed me to go to the window to register my name.

I thought to myself, "My goodness gracious! These guys brought with them their brown bag lunches. I wasn't informed that the wait will be this long. I might as well come back another day."

I was about to leave when I heard my name being called. I went quickly to the clerk's window.

"You're Evelyn Masaoy?"

"Yes, I am."

"Okay. Aside from the blood tests, your doctor wants a urinalysis. Here's a sterile bottle. Go to the ladies' toilet and fill it up with your urine specimen. Then wait to be called again." At this point she handed me a brown paper bag.

Lesson learned: *"You never know what's in a brown bag."*

# BEWARE: THIN AIR AHEAD!

Colorado is such a beautiful state! I visited it for the second time, with my son Jairus and his wife Christina, my daughter Bamba, and our friends Connie and Michelle.

We had been to the fabulous Garden of the Gods the previous day. The garden with its red rocks and rock formations was a fascinating natural work of art. It is another one of those wonders of the earth that was sculpted by the hands of God.

The Monument to America the Beautiful

This particular day we were to visit Pike's Peak. Jairus was to drive our van up that long and winding road to the summit. I had been there before. In fact I encouraged the group to ascend it in order to see for themselves what it was about this 14,000 foot summit that overwhelmed Katharine Lee Bates and inspired her to write the lyrics of the great patriotic

At the summit of Pike's Peak

song "America the Beautiful", the most famous and touching paean to this wonderful country, the U.S.A.

The view became increasingly marvelous as we continued to climb up the mountain. We knew we were near the summit when the evergreen trees started to thin out and then completely disappeared as we drove beyond the alpine level.

Getting off the van at the summit, we felt both relief and exhilaration. Relief, because the perilous drive was over; exhilaration, because the view up there was breathtaking.

No wonder this site had a profound impact on Ms. Lee Bates! No wonder, "America the Beautiful" was written on this mountain top!

The elevation, the strong winds, and the snow were too much for us. From the open air, we sought the comforting warmth of the visitors' center and souvenir shop. In here we settled on the most pleasant task of souvenir hunting. Then speaking half to myself and half to whoever could hear me, I said, "Why do I feel woozy?"

An elderly lady heard me and she replied, "Don't worry, that's a normal feeling at this elevation. You'll get over it in a while."

About a half hour later we were ready to pay for our purchases. Bamba stood in front of me at the line to the checkout counter. I noticed that she looked a bit pale. She, too, felt dizzy like the rest of us. A few seconds after she spoke to me, she gradually grew limp and was on the verge of collapsing. I called out for help. Within seconds two young EMT men rushed to her assistance. They carried her to the emergency treatment room where they seated her comfortably and gave her pure oxygen to breathe. After a few moments, her color returned. We were extremely grateful for the professional treatment by the EMT personnel. I thanked God that my daughter recovered so rapidly.

It was only then that we learned that there is such a thing as AMS or Acute Mountain Sickness, or simply, altitude sickness. This is said to be caused by the low partial pressure of oxygen in the air beginning at an altitude of 8,000 feet.

Having learned another lesson on travel, we left the awesome summit. We drove back down to sea level where the air is thicker and breathing is easier.

Lesson learned: *"Climbing up to the top may be a profound experience but could be hazardous to your health."*

❧ ❧

## HANKIES ARE NOT NECESSARILY FOR TEARS

The founder of the laboratory where I work was a very kind and pleasant Jewish gentleman, an immigrant from the USSR. When he died we naturally wanted to render our last respects. A group of us employees went to the funeral home. As soon as we walked in, each female was handed a round black lace cloth.

"This is really something. They're handing out lace hankies instead of Kleenex tissue paper," I said to myself.

I kept the lace cloth in my bag and thought nothing about it again.

In the course of the services I noticed that all the women had the lace cloth on top of their heads. I pulled the lace cloth from my bag, placed it on my head as I whispered to my friend who was seated beside me, "I thought those were for tears."

Lesson learned: *"Cultural differences matter."*

# THE SPELLING BEE CONTESTANT

Every three years since 1991, a group of friends whose common bond was our having been faculty members at the Faculty of Engineering, University of Santo Tomas in Manila, get together for a weekend of fun and reminiscing.

The following episode happened at a reunion in Washington D.C. when most of us were in our late fifties and early sixties. Probably the "Senior Moments" syndrome has started to be manifested by some of us.

Ofie to hotel operator: "Miss, can you please connect me to Mr. Rivera's room?"

Operator: "Mr. who?"

Ofie: "Mr. Rivera."

Operator: "Can you please spell that out for me, Ma'am."

Ofie: "Okay. R as in radio, A as in apple, D as in ..."

Operator: "Will you say that again, Ma'am?"

Ofie: "Okay, okay. R as in radio, A as in apple, D as in ... Okay, okay, erase, erase!"

And do you know that if she did not stop spelling, the next letter would have been "Y as in yo-yo"?

What Ofie was trying to spell out was "RADYO", the Filipino equivalent of radio. She completely forgot the "RIVERA" asked for by the operator. To this day, Ofie still can not fathom how the operator was able to come to terms with her. She somehow got her connected to Mr. Rivera's room!

Lesson learned: *"Listen to what you're saying."*

91

# THE GORILLA IS A TRULY BRAVE MAN

It was a very special September evening for Ray Zipagan. He was to be inducted as the new President of the University of Santo Tomas Engineering Alumni Association in the United States. The entire Zipagan clan led by Ray and his gracious wife, Melanie, together with a multitude of their mutual friends, had joined the alumni for the grand celebration. His 92-year old father Benito Zipagan honored his son by his participation in the festivities.

The guest speaker and inducting officer for that evening was Mr. Norman S. Karpf, a prominent New Jersey trial attorney. He spoke on the theme "Giving Back." His speech touched dramatically on Sgt. John Basilone, a great New Jersey Marine WWII hero, who set a profound example of not only giving back part of his time and treasure, but of giving back the ultimate of all gifts ... his life.

After Mr. Karpf's soul-stirring speech Ray approached our guest speaker to thank and congratulate him for the very meaningful and thought-provoking message which he delivered. Ray excused Mr. Karpf from our dinner table and then ushered him to another corner of the ballroom and passed people who were either dancing the night away or busy reminiscing about the olden days at their beloved alma mater.

The revelry went on amidst the noise of music and chatter. After a few minutes, Mr. Karpf came back with a very pleasant grin on his face. His usual formal gait has been transformed to one that looked like a child who had just been handed a red lollipop. He was visibly thrilled about something. Before he could reach our table he made a gesture asking me to meet him halfway across the hall. That was so unusual. Although I sensed his excitement, I reluctantly stood up saying to myself, "What, in heaven's name, is he up to?"

"Come with me. I would like you to meet a gorilla."

"What? ... A gorilla? A gorilla in this room? This must be a big joke." I looked at him with as much cynicism as I could muster.

Despite my disbelief at what I heard, I followed him to where a group of men were huddled together. I came face to face with a tall, lean, dignified elderly gentleman, exuding strength, bravery and intensity despite his 92 long years on this planet.

"Evelyn, I would like you to meet Ray's dad. I am very highly impressed by his role in your homeland during WWII. He was in the mountains of the Philippines during the dark days of that war when, for reasons unknown to them, the Filipino guerillas who were staunch allies of the United States in the war against Japan were left to fend for themselves, not only for food but for arms and ammunition, as well. General Douglas MacArthur, the American Commander in Chief in the Pacific Theater, whom they idolized as their leader, had been compelled to leave the country. It was primarily the General's resounding promise, spoken in three words, 'I shall return,' which reverberated throughout the archipelago, that enabled these courageous guerillas to continue their remarkable resistance against this relentless enemy."

"I am overwhelmed by the sacrifices of extreme danger, hunger, malnutrition and the dreadful malaria endured by this unforgettable patriot who sacrificed so much of himself for the Philippines and the United States."

Mr. Karpf went on and on with accolades to Ray's dad.

I stretched out my hand to shake the gentleman's hand as I humorously remarked. "I thought I was to meet a gorilla."

Far from being a gorilla ... the elder Mr. Zipagan is a brave Guerilla warrior who has served both the Philippines and the United States against the Japanese. No wonder, Mr. Karpf, who holds in great esteem the brave and selfless members of our military, was thrilled.

Stirring emotions arose within me as I realized how fortunate I was to meet my great countryman half-way around the world from our homeland.

Lesson learned: *"An encounter with a true hero awakens one's consciousness to the freedoms he helped preserve; freedoms which we still enjoy!"*

# WASABI

My brilliant thirteen-year-old granddaughter loves Japanese food much more than I do. She enjoys introducing me to the different specialties being served at the buffet table. She would take a bit of everything on a plate, taste each one, then tell me which ones are delicious. For dessert, she would do the same except for the ice cream which she puts in a cup. I saw several scoops of multi-colored ice cream in her cup. The scoop of green ice cream aroused my curiosity.

"Kiara, what are you eating?"

"Green tea ice cream, Grandma."

"Green tea ice cream! Sounds fascinating. I'll have some later."

Meanwhile, my sister Elena was on her way to get another serving of food, something she didn't really need. She overheard our conversation. When she came back she had a scoop of the green thing on her plate.

"I got some of this for you. You may take it from my plate."

"Thanks, but I'll just try a spoonful and you can have the rest."

I took a spoonful. Before I could say "green", I nearly choked. It was soooo spicy hot that I had to spit it out. It was wasabi, a hot, stinging, biting green condiment made of Japanese horseradish!

Lesson learned: *"Not all greens are pleasantly edible."*

# AN ISLAND'S JOURNEY FOR HALF A CENTURY

It was a real hot summer day in the Philippines in 1958 when my Mom and I left our rural hometown of Dao for the city of Manila. A couple of months before this I graduated valedictorian from Dao Catholic High School, the only secondary school in our area. My parents decided to send me to Manila where I was to study Chemical Engineering at the University of Santo Tomas, a prestigious Catholic university, the oldest university in the Far East.

Fast forward to February 2008. After thirty-one years residing in the suburbs of Manila as a student and then as an engineering professor at my Alma Mater, followed by nineteen years of residence in the U.S.A. where I am employed as a chemist in an environmental laboratory, I visited my hometown ... gray hair, wrinkles, flab, battle-scarred and all ... to attend the Golden Jubilee celebration of my high school graduation.

I looked forward with much anticipation and excitement to see my classmates after fifty long years.

One of our most memorable activities was a picnic by the beach; the same beach which we often visited and frolicked on during our younger days. We enthusiastically threw our flip-flops away. Some of us started playing with the waves, chasing them as they receded back to the sea, and running as fast as we could away from them as they pushed back their voluminous waters upon the beach. Others walked lazily on the beach, picking up marble-white pebbles, multi-colored pebbles or broken pieces of corals brought ashore by the waves. Some kept busy chasing the tiny 'crabbies' as they rushed back into the safety of their homes within the holes in the sand. It was like we were young again. We were re-living the past!

Amidst this fun and frolic I suddenly remembered one very beautiful spot: a barrio (hamlet) which was not too far from an island. The fascinating thing about the island at San Roque is that during low tide we could simply wade to it from the mainland.

"How far is San Roque from here?" I asked.

"Not too far. It's only about three kilometers away," replied Nema, a classmate who hails from there.

"Can we drive out there, please? I'd love to walk across the sea ... to that island ... once again.

"But of course, we can. But the island is gone."

"What do you mean by 'the island is gone'? Did it sink?"

"No, it did not sink. There's no more island. It's gone but it's not lost. Just wait 'till we get there."

"You're playing with me. C'mon, stop making a fool of me." My curiosity was building up.

"No, I'm serious. Just wait 'till we get there and you will understand."

I was puzzled by what Nema told me.

We parked our jeep some 300 meters from the beach at the edge of the curved trail which we used to trudge on. Nothing has changed ... it seemed.

Just before we reached the point where the trail made a sharp rightward turn, I caught a glimpse of the island. I was thrilled to see it. "C'mon, guys, I see the island now. Let's walk fast ... before the high tide catches us!" I yelled to the group.

"Yes, it's there. But it's an island no more." I tried to figure out what she meant, but I just could not comprehend it. No, not until we made that right turn. I was flabbergasted with what I saw.

During the fifty years that I have been away a strange geophysical evolution has occurred. A strip of land, about 100 meters wide has cropped out of the seabed, making a land bridge connecting the mainland and what used to be the island. Thus, the island is no longer an island.

I was filled with wonder as we walked over the land bridge to visit what used to be an island in my youth.

The renowned American author, Thomas Wolfe, may have referred to a phenomenon like this when he said, "You can't go home again."

Lesson learned: *"Fifty years' travel in time: if you're lucky you may experience minute but significant changes in the world around you."*

# THE IMPORTANCE OF ZERO

Ancestral home in La Paz, Iloilo City

Early February 2007 I went back to my hometown of Dao, Antique, Philippines for a four-day visit after which I had to fly back to Manila for the Centennial Celebrations of my alma mater. The trip by car from Dao to the airport in Iloilo City where I was to board my flight bound for Manila takes about two and a half hours, nonstop.

We left Dao early that morning. So much has changed along the route, especially as we approached the city. Many new huge and modern houses have been built since I left the country in 1989. But what interested me most along the way was the ancient but beautifully restored Catholic Church of Miagao which is now a UNESCO Heritage site. During my youth I often passed near this church but I have never gone out of my way to stop and enter. This time I did. The church's exquisite façade is more impressive than many of the churches I've seen around the world. In contrast, the interior is rather simple. We went inside and said a little prayer before going on our way.

There were a few errands to be done in Iloilo City. We had to pick up the pair of eye glasses which I ordered a week ago. Then we planned to pay a surprise visit to our two elderly cousins, Baby and Nang Melding, who still reside at the family's ancestral home in La Paz. We did surprise them with that unexpected visit. Since my flight was scheduled for 1:50 pm (so I thought), we decided to have lunch together at a local well-regarded restaurant. Food was at its best with the nationally famous La Paz *batchoy* (a kind of native noodle and meat soup)! We spent the few hours we had together catching up on news about the family.

We reached the airport at noon. I went straight to the counter to check in, only to get a shocking revelation from the desk clerk. "Ma'am your flight has left."

"What? My flight has left? How can that be? My flight is scheduled for 1:50 pm." I exclaimed.

"Well, Ma'am, you were booked for the flight at 10:50, not 01:50." I looked at my ticket ... and guess what! One zero is indeed "misplaced". For my stupidity, I had to shell out almost 600.00 Philippine pesos for me to get booked for the next flight to Manila.

Lesson learned: *"Zero is not always without value. It's relative location can make a considerable difference."*

# NEIGHBORS

The Tower of London

September 1990. I was in the USA for just a little more than a year. My sister Elena and I, both first time visitors to the magnificent aristocratic city of London, joined the long queue of tourists at the Tower of London for a glance at the famed Crown Jewels of the United Kingdom. The line was slow-moving. We happened to stand next to a couple who were evidently Americans. So we started conversing with them and soon learned that just like us they were from New Jersey. It struck a chord. We had something in common.

The curious New Jerseyan that I am asked, "So, where in New Jersey are you from?"

"Short Hills," was her reply.

"Where is that?" I asked.

"It's a part of Millburn," she replied.

My eyes lit up. "So we're neighbors."

"Why? Where are you from?"

"We do live close by ... a couple of towns away from you. We're from Irvington." I responded.

"O ... kay ... ," she answered. But I thought I heard some kind of unpleasant tinge in her voice.

"So, when do you plan to fly back home?" my sister asked.

"On Sunday," Mr. Short Hills replied. "We're flying by Concord."

Concord! My eyes widened in amazement. I was impressed.

"No wonder I was almost blinded by the sparkle of Mrs. Short Hills' diamond ring." I whispered in our Filipino dialect to my sister.

After we parted ways that day, we forgot the lively conversation until we got back to Irvington. I asked some friends where Short Hills was located. Only then did I know that Short Hills is one of the ritzy, glitzy parts of Northern New Jersey. No wonder! My proud response that we were neighbors from Irvington was acknowledged with an almost lifeless "Okay" which sounded more like a question asked with eyebrows raised rather than an affirmation.

I was too naive then to know that delineations existed between the poor apartments and littered streets of Irvington versus the manicured lawns of the glittering mansions of Short Hills. I was naively proud to declare that I, too, lived in New Jersey ... Irvington, NJ. That town, too, is in the U.S.A. isn't it?

Lesson learned: *"Know thy neighbor!"*

# DRIVE RIGHT

"We are taking a bus to Oxford. We're staying there 'till Monday." That was Elsie's surprise for us as she greeted my sister and I at Heathrow Airport for our week-long stay in England.

University of Santo Tomas, Manila

"But isn't that a school?" I asked. "How can we sleep there?"

"A school? Yes and no," she replied, amused at my obvious ignorance. "Oxford is a city where the famous Oxford University, the oldest university in the English-speaking world, is located."

"Did you say the oldest university? What about my alma mater, the University of Santo Tomas in Manila, Philippines, founded in 1611? Isn't that the oldest university, older than any university in the USA; older than Harvard, 1636, or Yale, 1701?"

Radcliffe Camera, Oxford

"Yes, UST is the oldest university in Asia, as well as older than any university in the USA. But Oxford's date of establishment isn't even clear. Around the year 1096 teaching was already taking place there; but its growth as a learning institution became evident in 1167."

"Wow! That's a big lesson in history for me. All these years I had the impression that UST is the oldest university in the world."

I started to become cognizant of the larger world ... much larger than the little country where I hail from.

The next morning we were enthralled by the sight of the magnificent spires of Oxford, the Radcliffe Camera, and the million other things which make Oxford ... Oxford.

Before Elena and I left for our tour of the city, Elsie gave us instructions as to where to go and what to see. "Most important of all", she emphasized, "at the end of the day, take a taxi, give our home address and don't worry, the driver will just take you there."

Dusk came. Time to head back to one of the ancient buildings in the heart of the city. It was called the Old Palace. We hailed a cab, spoke to the driver and gave our address. He asked us to hop in. Not willing to miss any interesting sites along the way, I decided to take the front seat. My sister sat in the back. I went around to the right side front door and opened it. "Madam, do you plan to drive?" That was the driver's funny way of telling me. "You idiot, you're in England. We drive right."

"Oh, oh," was all I could say as I ran around to the other side.

Walking the streets of Oxford in 1990

Lesson learned: *"Left? Right? Know where you stand."*

# THERE'S TROUBLE UP THERE

It was late in the evening when we came out of the Theatre Royal in London. My sister and I had a great time watching Miss Saigon, more especially so because Lea Salonga, a *kababayan* (fellow Filipino), played the lead role.

We were to take the underground back to our temporary "house" in Surrey. When we reached the underground station we looked for signs for the train that would take us to Surrey. This being our first time to travel in London by ourselves, we got confused. So we approached a gentleman and I asked, "Sir, my sister and I need to take the train to Surrey. Do we wait for it here or do we go to the upper level?"

"Madam, if you go to the upper level, you'll be in great trouble. You don't play Fiddler on the Roof, do you?"

As it turned out, we were already on the top level of that station.

Lesson learned: *"Beware of climbing to the top. It may bring you nowhere."*

"Twenty years from now you
will be more disappointed by
the things you didn't do
than by the ones you did do.

So throw off the bowlines,
sail away from the safe harbor.
Catch the trade winds in your sails.
Explore.  Dream.  Discover."

Mark Twain

# AN ISLAND CAN'T WAIT

We were cruising through the picturesque Inner Passage in Alaska. Early one afternoon we were in our cabin where some of us decided to steal a few winks. I was looking out from my bunk when I noticed that we were passing beside some not too distant island. The view was simply gorgeous.

I called Nelia who was starting to doze off on her bunk below mine. "Nelia, there's a beautiful view. You wouldn't want to miss this. Come on, take a picture of it."

Sleepily, she replied, "Okay, I'll take that picture tomorrow."

"Duh!"

Lesson learned: *"Take that picture now for you may not pass this way again ..."*

🐾🐾

# WHERE EAST MEETS WEST

Time was when we truly believed that "East is east and West is west and never the twain shall meet."

Juneau, Alaska was one of the stops during our 2006 cruise which brought us on a ride through the fantastic Inner Passage.

Juneau, the capital of Alaska, was founded during a gold rush in 1880. Nestled at the foot of Mt. Juneau, this former gold mining town is situated in one of Alaska's most spectacular scenic locations. Our group went for a ride on the Mount Roberts Cable Car, not only to have an awesome view of the city, but also to experience the wholesome smell of fresh clean air on the mountain top. During the ascent of the cable car, we caught sight of a baby bear. Before long, a park police officer came to assure tourists that all is safe.

We hiked up the mountain where we met another group of tourists from another cruise ship. We enjoyed exchanging pleasantries and experiences with them. The view from the top was fantastic!

The city commercial center at the foot of the mountain was waiting for us to come down and do some souvenir shopping. As we walked around the city, our attention was caught by a building emblazoned with conspicuously large letters ... "Filipino Community Center."

"What? A Filipino Community Center in the heart of Alaska?" We chorused. We were astounded. We entered the building and were warmly greeted by a group of fellow Filipinos. They are proud citizens of Juneau.

"Wow! We are really surprised to learn that there is an active Filipino community here. How long have you folks been here? All your life? That's amazing!" We excitedly blurted out these questions to a 60-year-old Filipino gentleman who was enjoying his late breakfast of *tinapa at sinangag,* a very typical Filipino meal.

Several other elderly compatriots joined in our conversation. After listening to their stories they asked us if we had visited the city square. They strongly suggested that we go there. They did not tell us why. "We want you to be surprised with what you will see." That was their way of encouraging us to see the square for ourselves.

So, off to the city square we went. To our great surprise the area bounded by S. Franklin St., Admiral Way, and Marine Way was a plaza called Manila Square. A bust of Jose Rizal, the Filipino national hero, is proudly enshrined in this very special site, right in the heart of Juneau. It was dedicated to honor the Filipinos who settled here as early as 1788 and were co-founders of this city. It also recognized all the Filipino inhabitants of Juneau who are active and valued members of the community.

Clearly, the East did meet West in this far corner of the globe. Who would have expected it?

Lesson learned: *"A surprise always lurks for a traveler. Yes, even in the farthest corners of the earth!"*

# BEYOND OUR DREAMS

In the Canadian Rockies one rocky mountain range ends where another glacier-topped mountain begins. There seems to be an endless flow of awesome sights; a kind of natural beauty that makes your heart skip several beats. The views make your mind explode in wonder and in heightened admiration of the natural sculpture which only the hand of the Almighty could create. These are the sceneries which cause you to cry out emphatically ... "Oh, my God! What boundless beauty!" ... and really mean it from the depths of your being,

I have seen a minuscule sample of an ice sculpture; the kind used to decorate a food-laden table for some lavish feast. This particular day we did not only see but we were standing on one of these humongous ice sculptures of Mother Nature. Estela, Nelia, Bel and I joined the Columbia Icefield Glacier Adventure. We boarded a Brewster Ice Explorer, a jumbo bus specially designed for glacial travel which drove atop the glacier. We got off the bus and started our personal glacier adventure.

Holding on to each other, Bel, Nelia, and I walked on that mega ice sculpture carefully and slowly, fearful that we might slip and slide. Then we went to a higher elevation where water was dripping droplets of melted ice which we collected in the cups of our hands. We drank a handful of glacier water. What an extraordinary treat! All four of us were born and raised in the hot tropical islands of the Philippines where, as children, the only ice we saw were those tiny blocks floating on a glass of water or soda; the only snow we saw was the frost in the freezer before frost-free refrigerators were invented.

Did any of us ever dream of walking on top of a glacier? Did we ever think of riding on a huge bus on a roadway on top of a glacier? Did we ever foresee that we could take a sip of melted glacier from the cups of our hands? Did we know that the surface of the glacier is grayish with dust and not as white as snow? No, we never dreamed of any of them. In fact we never knew that the glacier could be within our reach. But it was! And that was one of the most fascinating experiences on this trip.

Lesson learned: *"Travel and reach beyond your dreams."*

# GOING BILINGUAL HAS ITS DOWNSIDE TOO

There were seven in our tour group on a cruise to New Brunswick and Nova Scotia, Canada. This particular day we had a shore excursion and tour of St. John, New Brunswick, the place known as the "Greatest Little City in the East".

We were on Prince William street. Photo "maniacs" that we all were; we rushed to cross the city street when we saw a funny-looking statue which is the landmark of that area. Baybee, a good-humored young lady, was left behind waiting for all of us to cross and pose so that she could take our group

Baybee (in green) catching up with the rest of the group

picture. A young man approached her from behind and offered to take the picture himself so that Baybee could join us.

Baybee, fearing to entrust her camera to a stranger who might have a "fast slight of hand", reluctantly handed over her valuable possession containing hundreds of precious pictures taken during previous days, as she muttered in an audible voice. *"Naku, baka i-takbo ng mama ang camera ko!"* ("Oh my gosh, this man might run away with my camera!")

Whereupon the man immediately replied, *"Tama ka. Sigue, itatakbo ko ito."* ("You're right, I'll run away with this.")

Oops! Only then did she realize that the good Samaritan was a fellow Filipino who not only fully understood what she said, but even responded in the same language. Baybee felt embarrassed, but being the funny lady that she is, she was able to convert the embarrassing situation to a really funny one! They exchanged humor for a few moments, thereby creating a relaxed atmosphere.

Lesson learned: *"Going bilingual has its downside, too."*

# NATURE'S MAGIC

Medicine Lake

Medicine Lake is one of the most unusual lakes we visited in the Jasper National Park in Canada. The aboriginal people who lived beside the lake gave it the name "Big Medicine" which means "magic". They feared this lake because of its magical behavior. In summer it looks like any other lake with no visible outlets. But by September the water level begins to recede. The lake disappears by October and leaves behind only some potholes amid mudflats for the rest of the year. Then the cycle repeats.

This phenomenon has baffled the natives for years. They attributed it to spirits and supernatural beings. They believed that the lake had paranormal powers.

It would have been more exciting to preserve the mystery and wonder of such an inexplicable occurrence in nature. But that was not to be so.

Scientific studies and investigations have completely demolished this magic and mystery.

The explanation goes this way: There is a network of underground passages called sinkholes in the bedrock beneath the lake. We might envision these as a series of caves. In October, when the temperature begins to drop and the glaciers stop melting, the little amount of water remaining in the lake sinks into this network. Thus the lake disappears. In summer, the water from the melted snow and glaciers is of such a volume that the underground network cannot hold. Hence, the overflow goes out to the surface and the lake reappears.

Amazing! But, see what scientific education can do? It erases the awe and excitement we feel for natural mysteries.

Lesson learned: *"Nature exists. Science explains why."*

# PANDA GLACIER

If someone asks me where I have seen the most beautiful sceneries among the places I have visited so far, I ask back, "Nature-made or man-made?"

If you want nature, I have one sure answer: the Canadian Rockies.

It was a warm cloudless sunny day in July 2007. We were driving from Maligne Lake back to our hotel in Canmore. We had run out of superlative expressions with which to cry out our admiration for the God-given wonders with which this majestic mountain range has been blest. This place has been gifted with so much natural beauty that anywhere you turn beauty emanates from every nook and cranny.

I remember the zigzag road where we made a brief stop at a lookout where we viewed the roadway far below. This same winding road is where we will drive down from this mountain top, then on to the level highway. Even this human engineering marvel is no match for the profusion of natural elegance that surrounded us.

Nelia was driving at a leisurely pace. We were headed for home, so why hurry? The shimmering white caps on the towering mountain tops could be seen with nary a cloud to block the view. Then something very unusual caught our attention. We saw this majestic glacier topped mountain looming before us in the shape of a humongous panda. Yes, a glacier that looks like a ... P-p-p-panda!

As we drove closer and closer to it there was one moment

when it even looked like a panda with sun glasses. Estela was able to capture the unusual phenomenon with her camera. The tiny scientific voice within me explained it as a result of the interplay of snow, rocks, lights, and shadows. But the spiritual part of me couldn't help exclaiming, "Oh. God what an astonishing sight! Unbelievable! Extraordinary! Awesome! Thank you, God, thank you!"

That was one magical moment which will probably never ever be seen again.

Lesson learned: *"Travel and capture each magical moment!"*

⚡⚡

## RIGHT OF WAY

Estela, Nelia, and the Author at Lake Minnewanka

July 6, 2007. We were in Alberta, Canada. Our destination was Lake Minnewanka, called "Lake of the Water Spirits" by the Aborigines, then later on called "Devil's Lake" by the early Europeans. It is said that this place has been revered and feared by residents and visitors for over 10,000 years. I tried to find out why this magnificent lake has been given names which evoke this feeling of fear despite the fact that there was nothing fearsome about the area. I couldn't get a plausible explanation. Be that as it may, we simply enjoyed the majestic scenery as we climbed the whitish boulders at the edge of the lake so as to get a better picture of the vicinity.

The lake is too huge for a few minutes stay. The entire 20 kilometer stretch may be explored by an hour long cruise. But that would have taken too much of our time. After a few minutes visit, we drove on to our next destination.

Not far from the lake we were surprised by the very slow pace of vehicular traffic on a seemingly deserted highway. It wasn't long before we knew the answer. We saw a ram at the edge of the roadway. We slowed down as we observed him observing us. He looked immobile as he sat watching the vehicles go by while proudly showing off his huge pair of curled horns which together made the shape of a graceful "M" over his head.

A few meters behind the ram there was a herd of wild animals ... mountain goats, I think ... walking nonchalantly in the middle of the road. They owned the road! We stopped, as all other motorists did. Vehicular traffic was at a complete standstill. Meanwhile, cameras kept clicking as we enjoyed watching this parade of animals. No vehicle moved until the entire herd had disappeared back into the wild. No doubt, they had the right of way!

Lesson learned: *"Yield to nature!"*

# THE WHOLE IS BIGGER THAN THE
# SUM OF ITS PARTS

Spirit Island

As it turned out, July is the best time of the year to visit the numerous parks in the Canadian Rockies.

We made a brief stop at the small but beautiful town of Jasper. From there we drove to Maligne Lake. We saw lots of elk and deer along the way. We parked near the Maligne Lake Ticket Office, visited their souvenir shop, had lunch, and made ourselves ready for the cruise to Spirit Island. Even before we boarded our tour boat, the view before us was awesome.

The elegance of the snow capped mountains towering on both sides of the lake, heightened by the luxuriant evergreens, presented an endless photographer's treat. The view and the travel were enhanced by the beauty of the human spirit. I noticed that even on the lake, the cruise boat captains observed what I called the "Lake Traffic Code of Courtesy". As soon as the bigger boat saw a much smaller boat or a raft along its way it immediately slowed down in the course of overtaking the smaller boat or raft.

Before reaching Spirit Island we were informed that this is one of the most photographed sceneries in this part of the globe.

Spirit Island is a very tiny piece of land, so small that there are only about a dozen or so evergreens crowded on its whole area. Alone, it was most insignificant. By itself it was nothing at all.

What made it spectacular was how its diminutive presence stood out amidst the towering snow capped mountains which surrounded it. It seemed to float on the serene turquoise waters of the lake. It was only when you looked at the island as part of the whole that you realized the magnificence of the total scenery before you. The whole looked tremendously greater than the sum of all its parts! God! What a sight! What a marvel of your creation . . . the work of your hands!

Lesson learned: *"The whole is bigger than the sum of its parts."*

# TOO MANY MOUNTAINS TO POLICE

It was a gorgeous, clear, lovely day in July. We were in the middle of the Canadian Rockies. This is a place where nature's beauty is at its best. Nothing could be better than the view of nature here. We were driving from Canmore to the Banff National park.

Dazzling snow-capped mountains, shimmering glaciers, towering trees, emerald-colored lakes ... they're everywhere. We were not only enjoying the spectacular scenery. We were fooling around with our imaginations as we compared the shapes of the mountains to mansions, and of the glaciers to human faces. Bel suddenly jolted us out of our reverie with the down to earth question: "There are so many mountains here. But where are the mountain police? I haven't seen any."

Estela, a Canadian, responded, "Bel, there's no mountain police that I know of. Do you mean the Royal Mounted Police? You'll see them at the parade when we get to Calgary!"

Lesson learned: *"Watch out for what you hear and say. Some words do 'sound like' but don't necessarily 'mean like'."*

# A JOURNEY INTO A ROSE GARDEN

"A rose is a rose is a rose." This is a line from the classic poem entitled Sacred Emily, written by Gertrude Stein.

A rose is a rose is a r .... ? No, a rose is a rose and goes beyond being simply a rose.

We visited Butchart Gardens in Victoria, British Columbia. This complex of numerous gardens is situated on fifty-five acres of rich soil, profusely blooming a rainbow of colors in spring and in summer.

Going back to a brief history of these gardens, my admiration for this grandiose achievement of Robert Pim and Jennie Butchart became even more profound. This couple acted as a team. While Robert's endeavors caused him to dig out the limestone deposits for his Portland Cement industry which left an enormous hole in the ground, Jennie conceived a great idea which turned that pit into a spectacular Sunken Garden.

What would have been an eyesore of an abandoned quarry was gradually turned into a Japanese Garden in 1909, followed by an Italian garden, and a Rose Garden. Then rows of evergreens and innumerable species of flowering plants were planted around fountains, ponds, and lawns in a park-like atmosphere.

The Rose Garden itself was started in 1929 on what was originally the Butchart's vegetable garden. It is now a home to 6,600 varieties of roses which surround an oval lawn.

As you enter the Rose Garden you walk on a pathway overarched with blossoms of climbing roses. Then you find yourself literally surrounded by a sea of roses. I sat down on the rose garden curb for a few moments. All my senses were awash with the hues, the scent, the sound of the blossoms as they swayed with the wind. Only my sense of taste was unable to participate in that experience. What the taste could not do was superseded by what my mind did in its stead.

"What makes a rose stand out in a sea of flowers?" I asked myself.

"Because a rose represents love and life," a voice within me answered.

Contemplating further upon the Creator's work of art, my mind wandered throughout the rose garden.

Isn't a rose symbolic of life and love? Its gorgeous beauty entices you. Its irresistible call propels you in its direction. Attracted by its loveliness, you gladly embrace it: blossoms, leaves, stems and thorns.

Yes, thorns! Roses come with thorns. They wound, they hurt; you suffer and you bleed. The analogy to life and love is evident.

Lesson learned: *"As unto the rose, the thorn is; so unto life and love, the toils and the struggles are."*

# CATHARSIS

The small tourist bus carrying about 15 tourists from the business center of Mexico City was headed for the Basilica of Our Lady of Guadalupe. I came as a tourist and not a pilgrim.

I have read about the miracle which happened in Tepeyac in 1531. I knew how the Blessed Virgin Mary appeared to Juan Diego, a peasant native American; how the Bishop at that time disbelieved Juan Diego; how on December 12 of that year, in the

The *tilma* enshrined in the Basillica of Our Lady of Guadalupe

freezing snow of winter and beside the spot where the Blessed Mother again appeared, Juan Diego found a rose bush in full bloom; how he carried the blossoms in his *tilma,* brought them to Bishop Zumarraga as a proof of Juan Diego's truthfulness; how the Blessed Mother miraculously left her image on the *tilma;* and how this image was unknowingly displayed to the bishop when Juan Diego presented the rose blossoms to him.

The *tilma* of Saint Juan Diego is enshrined in the basilica which was our destination.

During the drive our guide mentioned to us numerous facts of which I was unaware at that time. She told us that the *tilma* has been scientifically studied numerous times, and that scientific results could not explain the findings. Here are some which I clearly remember:

1. The *tilma* which is made of maguey cactus fibers has a normal lifespan of 20 to 30 years. Yet, Juan Diego's tilma, which is almost 500 years old, shows no sign of disintegration.
2. Regardless of the room and ambient temperature, the *tilma*

remains at a constant temperature of 98.6° Fahrenheit, the normal body temperature.

3. When you are 3 to 4 inches from the colored image you won't see any color; you will only see the fibers.
4. There are no brush strokes on the "painted" image. Analysis of the "paint" revealed that its composition does not belong to any known element.
5. Laser ray tests reveal that the color hovers at 1/100 of an inch over the cloth.
6. Medical eye specialists who examined the Lady's eye found that it has the characteristics of the human eye.
7. Digital technology which has the capability of immensely enlarging an image, discovered that the eyes contain the figure of Juan Diego opening the *tilma* before Bishop Zumarraga.
8. The stars on Our Lady's mantle give the exact configuration of the stars on December 12, 1531.

As I listened intently to these salient facts, I recognized the presence of a two-fold miracle. The apparition of the Blessed Mother to Juan Diego was overwhelming. The *tilma* itself is another major miracle. Beyond these miracles, and of utmost importance, is the Blessed Mother's message of love and protection to the Americas: "Am I not here, I, who am your Mother?"

Shortly thereafter the bus came to a stop. We found ourselves in the wide open hilly part of Mexico City. We were directly in front of what appeared to be a huge circular edifice topped with a beautiful crown surmounted by a clearly defined letter M and a cross. "We are now in front of the Basilica of Our Lady of Guadalupe. I will give you one hour to explore on your own. Please be back on time." That was our guide giving us the usual instructions.

Being seated near the door, I was the first to alight from the bus. As soon as I set foot on the ground, a strange ... very, very strange ... feeling enveloped me. I felt a kind of warmth ... pleasant ... but strange. Then I started to cry. I had no reason to cry. But I did. Unstoppable tears came rushing out of my eyes, falling down my cheeks. I was sobbing with sobs coming from the depths of my being. I desperately searched for a tissue in my bag. And like a big joke, it took me some time to find the tissue which hid itself beneath the variety of junk in a woman's purse.

This catharsis continued for a good five minutes or so. Perhaps, having learned more about the miracle, I was deeply touched by the supernatural and heavenly event which occurred here. The catharsis turned my visit into a pilgrimage.

Lesson learned: *"Holy Mary, mother of God, pray for us sinners."*

⚜ ⚜

## BLANKETS OF TEOTIHUACAN

Pyramid of the Moon

Our weekend trip to Mexico brought us to Zocalo which became our home base and from where we took one day trips to nearby tourist destinations. One of the day trips brought us around Mexico City itself, then on to Teotihuacan. Here we ventured up close to the ruins of an ancient civilized world. From the pictures we have seen it seemed like climbing to the top of the Pyramid of the Moon and the Pyramid of the Sun were easy things do to. After all there were steps. And so what's the big deal about going up those steps?

Estela and I shared the excitement of the entire bus load of tourists with whom we were traveling. The ambitious plan was to get to the top of either or both the Pyramid of the Moon and the Pyramid of the Sun. After our guide had brought us around the ruins of some of the very impressive ceremonial, social and residential edifices, we were given time to explore by ourselves the other parts of this pre-Hispanic urban, mythical and ancient metropolis.

We approached the Pyramid of the Moon first. To our dismay, we found out that not only was the inclination uncomfortably too steep, but that the steps were uneven. Some were wide; some were narrow and high. So we decided to simply walk from one ruin to another, taking a close look at each one. We could not help but be very much impressed by the sophisticated engineering know-how of these Mezoamericans. They were truly astonishingly ahead of their time.

Our walk among the ruins on the broad north-south road called the Avenue of the Dead gave opportunity for the hawkers to approach us with their goods. Estela and I, both being homemakers, were mesmerized by the quality and the beauty of the colorful hand woven blankets. We went through the haggling process from the initial quote of $100.00 down to $15.00. We were pleased with our negotiating skills. Before long another blanket vendor approached us. His goods were more beautiful. So we went through the haggling process once again. Eventually, we had our hands full with two heavy blankets each.

We suddenly realized that we had barely five minutes to get back to our bus for the ride to the next destination. But the bus stop was like a 15 minute walk. So we started to run. Nevertheless we were still late. The bus driver saw us running from a distance and was relieved to know that we were on our way.

We were embarrassed because a whole bus load of fellow tourists was waiting for us. We apologized profusely for our tardiness.

Then as we took our seats someone at the back of the bus said, "You ladies sure enjoyed your shopping, didn't you?" It was not so much what he said but how he said it that made us feel guilty for being late.

Lesson learned: *"Time is of the essence."*

# LIRA IS NOT REAL

One of the things I really wanted to take home from Brazil was an authentic Brazilian made pair of shoes. So I went out to shop for them in Rio de Janeiro. I couldn't understand the sign written in front of every pair on the display shelves. I learned later on that it indicated the amount payable for each partial payment and the number of payments to be made.

Since I still had some local currency on hand, I asked the shopkeeper how much the pair costs. He said, "Sixty dollars."

"No, not dollars," I said. "I want to pay in Lira."

"No Lira, you pay dollars," he insisted.

I pulled my local currency out of my purse and showed it to him. "I want to pay in Lira, your money. Look, here's what I have." The man laughed. "Senora, this no Lira. This ... Real ... Brazil money. Good. I take."

Then I realized that Lira is for Italy as Real is for Brazil!

Brazil's Real

Italy's Lira

Lesson learned: *"Know your currency. Lira is not Real."*

# PUBLIC PHONE SERVICE IN THE ANDES

Up in the Andes in the town of Urcos, in Peru, Gabriel our tour bus driver stopped at the town plaza. He excused himself for a few minutes explaining that he had to make a phone call to their main office. He said that he was going to use a "public phone". Interestingly this was how it went: There were people standing in the town plaza, each with a cell phone in hand. For a fee, they will allow anyone to use the phone to make a call.

That, my friends, is the public phone system in the mountains of the Andes.

Lesson learned:   *"Man versus machine: Man's limitless capability overrides the machine's limitations."*

# HIKING ON THE RAILROAD TRACKS

Machu Picchu, Peru

Machu Picchu, Peru, also known as the Lost City of the Incas, is a UNESCO World Heritage Site. Rightly so. It is undoubtedly a grand showcase of the engineering and architectural mastery and skill of the Incas.

Aguas Calientes is a small town that serves the tourist industry of Peru, specifically those who come to visit the wonders of the Lost City. This town is situated at the end of the rail line which is the beginning of the bus route that carried us to the Lost City.

Our schedule had set aside one extra day for this town. We wanted to make full use of our time.

It was a toss-up between the Hot Springs and the Water Falls near the city center of Aguas Calientes. The Hot Springs, I guess, were farther than the Falls. The problem was that nobody could give us the exact distance from the "pueblo" to either destination. The misinformation varied from a two-hour walk, one way, to 45 minutes. Hoping it was 45 minutes to the Falls, the unanimous decision was to walk to Mandor Falls.

Another problem arose ... which route do we take? The natives' reply was, "Follow the railroad."

"But there's no road parallel to the railroad." There was obvious concern in our voices.

"That's okay, the railroad will take you to the Falls."

"You mean, we will walk on the railroad?"

"Yes."

"Isn't it dangerous?"

"No, everybody does it."

So despite all the warnings posted along the tracks, "Danger! Don't walk on the tracks!", off we went, walking on the rails, on the wooden planks, or beside the rails; transferring from one side to the other, whichever had a wider shoulder; ready to jump off ... just in case a train comes chug-chugging along. At one point, I looked down the cliff and saw a road running parallel to the railroad. I suggested that we might be able to go down and walk on the road. I was overruled. And so ... on ... over ... beside ... the railroad tracks ... we edged our way.

Walking on the railroad tracks

Oh, those stones between planks and on the railroad bed mercilessly thrust themselves against our feet! Our shoes were not designed for such a rough roadbed. It was tiring, exhausting, and extremely hurting to the feet. ... But there was no turning back.

It turned out to be a fascinating hike. Along the way we met fellow travelers who were coming back from the Falls. They were adventurers, young and old, from various parts of the world including Germany, Spain, Italy, France, Israel, and Kazakhstan. We got into some animated and friendly, although brief, conversations with them.

"Did you all walk on the railroad, too?" We asked.

"But of course, we did. Just be sure to move over to the side when you hear a train coming. Enjoy!"

Lesson learned:
*"When in Peru do as the Peruvians do."*

Trekkers meet on the railroad tracks

# THE TWENTY-FIRST CENTURY INCAS

The Terraces of Ollantaytambo

Frustration takes over when you arrive at a world renowned site and expect to meet the challenges presented but fail to do so because your physical strength is sapped as you are mesmerized by the wonders before you.

This happened to members of our tour group when we reached Ollantaytambo in Peru. This is known as the Sacred Valley of the Incas. The town is located at the foot of some magnificent terraces on top of which is the temple of the Incas. This is another monumental legacy of the Incan civilization. As we approached the terraces, we thought the climb would be a piece of cake. Reaching the top looked attainable.

So ... up the terraces we climbed following our agile guide, Vida, who was effortlessly and gracefully gliding from one terrace to another.

I don't know how many terraces there were, but after climbing up seven of them, Estela complained about her fear of heights. Violy could not go further up because her sleepless nights in the high altitude of the city of Cusco had weakened her. Me? I felt that I couldn't catch my breath if I continued to climb.

So ... while the rest of the group continued their ascent, the three of us started our descent ... back to the base ... where we rested our tired and breathless selves and waited for our companions to rejoin us.

From where we were seated, we had a clear view of the climbers on the terraces to our right and a mountain to our left. We wondered how the Incas carved the Inca King's crowned head at the edge of that distant and high mountain, so much like our four great presidents' sculptures at Mt. Rushmore which were carved out of the mountains of South Dakota. Did Gutzon Borglum know about this Incan architectural achievement when he embarked on his project here in the USA? Between the years 1200 when the Inca tribes were believed to have existed and 1927 when the United States Congress approved the construction of the sculptures upon Mt. Rushmore, was there any linkage between the mountain sculptors of Manco Inca and President Calvin Coolidge?

Our questions remain unanswered.

As the "conquerors" of the temple gathered back at our base, we had good news for them.

"Guys, look! In your absence we have earned an honorary membership to the Inca tribe. It was a fierce fight we had to undergo in order to deserve the citizenship. We had a hard time convincing them that we rightly deserve the name. Finally the chief relented and gave the three of us the title ... 'Twenty First Century INCA-pables' ... for being incapable of reaching the temple at the top of the terraces."

Thus were we called "INCA-pables" for the remainder of the tour!

The Inca King's crowned head

Lesson learned: *"A title earned is a title deserved."*

# WILLY'S BITTER PERUVIAN COFFEE

Still in Peru, we were driving from the high altitude of Cusco to Raqchi where we visited the ruins of the Wari civilization. Here we walked through what remained of their pre-Incan engineering and architecture. This settlement dates back to about 700 B.C. or about 500 to 600 years before Incan culture. Within the walled city there were circular granaries (to store dehydrated potatoes in particular), temples and buildings constructed from mortars made of clay, straw and human hair. The walls and some structures were made from igneous rocks. They were provided with protruding stones that served as "Wari elevators" according to our guide's humorous remarks.

Although we enjoyed that part of the trip, some of us were still feeling the discomfort caused by the extreme elevation of Cusco. We were pleased to learn that we were driving towards a much lower altitude.

Most of us felt better when we stopped for lunch at La Pascana, a lovely rustic eatery slightly downhill from the highway. The railroad was a few meters away and the distant mountains were clearly visible from there. The transparent glass walls of the restaurant allowed us an unobstructed view of the alpacas, horses, llamas, and goats grazing in the open fields surrounding the restaurant.

Still wobbly due to Cusco's altitude, Estela's husband, Willy, the only knight with a group of seven ladies, needed his cup of coffee desperately. He quickly added cream and sugar to the steaming brew, mixed it and took a big sip. Meanwhile, I was lazily mixing my own coffee.

"Evelyn, how's your coffee?" He asked.

I took a sip from my cup. "My coffee is excellent. Very freshly brewed, I suppose."

"Mine tastes strange. It seems bitter. I don't really understand the taste. I wonder if that's how strong Peruvian coffee really tastes." He took a sip again. Then he picked up a container full of white powder with the intention of adding more sugar into his cup. It was labeled "SALT".

Lesson learned: *"Labels are there for a purpose."*

# THE WATERS OF LAKE TITIKAKA

Santa Maria Island on Lake Titikaka

Rene, our guide, explained that we were going to Uros, a group of about 44 artificial islands on Lake Titikaka, a lake that is partly in Peru and partly in Bolivia. Titi means Puma; kaka means gray or stone. The lake is believed to have the shape of a puma catching a rabbit; hence, the name Titikaka. It is the highest navigable lake in the world. Four rivers feed the lake and one river flows out of it.

We were driven a few blocks from the hotel to the wharf where we took a boat for the trip to these incredible man-made islands. Yes, you read it right! These are man-made rather than natural islands!

Upon arriving at Santa Maria Island we were welcomed by colorfully clad natives called Uros whose culture came before the Incas. We were then made to sit comfortably on reed benches as Rene delivered his very interesting and educational lecture on how to make an artificial island.

Totora reeds and eucalyptus branches are the raw materials for island making. The reed is divided into four parts: the "kili" or the root; the "chuyo" or the soft white part which is edible and can be eaten raw after the outer fiber is removed or which may be opened up, flattened and applied to one's forehead to relieve a headache; the reed itself which is the consumable part, eaten by animals or made into the island surface or "ground" and everything on it; and the flower which is a medicine for stomachache and menopause. Totora reeds grow abundantly in Lake Titikaka.

The root part is about 2.5 meters high. Reeds are taken from their habitat and blocks of roots are cut. Eucalyptus branches are inserted in the middle of that small block. Four such blocks are put together, the branches tied together to make a bigger block. It takes about 2 to 3 months for the blocks to bond together as a single piece.

The process is repeated until you get to the size of the island you want to build. Reeds 3 to 4 meters long are then laid on top of each other on a crisscross pattern across the island. This is done until you have about 2.5 meters thickness from the root surface. The island is anchored to the lake by eucalyptus branches.

It takes at least 8 months to build an island. Houses also made of reeds sit on top of the reed-island-floor. During summer new layers of reeds are placed on the island. Ironically, dried reeds are also used for fuel. One wonders how the islands don't catch fire.

Samples of chuyo, freshly peeled, were passed around for us to taste. It was good. It tasted like the coconut palm heart. We also tried putting the opened chuyo to our foreheads. Its cold watery sap was very refreshing. Then I was "honored" to receive a bunch of totora flowers.

The curious among us asked, "Where do the natives take a bath?"

"In the lake, naturally." Some of us volunteered the answer. Rene agreed.

"Where do they do their laundry?"

"In the lake." Rene replied.

"Where do they throw their garbage?"

"In the lake, too. You see, the reeds serve as filters."

"Okay, we understand. But ... where do they pee?"

"Into the lake."

The next question remained unasked. We knew the answer.

Neither did anyone dare to ask where they get their cooking and drinking water from.

We were certain of the answer.

Lesson learned:  *"Nature and man together take care of each other."*

# PROUD TO BE AMERICANS

A group of us, tourists from the USA, were walking the semi-dark streets of Cusco, Peru, on our way to an 8:00 p.m. dinner. We were chattering in our Filipino dialect as we walked.

Thinking that we were Japanese, a group of friendly-looking locals tried to catch our attention by saying some Japanese words. We ignored them. So they walked in step with us.

"Japanese?" One asked.

"No," we replied.

"Chinese?"

"No."

"Korean?"

"No."

"Vietnamese?"

"No."

They went on and on, mentioning more Asian countries except the Philippines.

Eventually, I said aloud to them, "We are Americans!"

They looked at us with quizzical looks on their faces.

"Oh, Americans! Welcome to Peru!" Then they walked away and left us alone.

In my mind, these young people must have found some kind of a "disconnect" there.

Perhaps in their minds they were saying, "Americans? But they all look Asian."

Lesson learned:  *"Proud to be Americans!  Yes, indeed!"*

## WHAT DIFFERENCE CAN A TRIPOD MAKE?

Royal Palace, Madrid, Spain

Can someone please explain this to me?

A couple of friends and I were standing on the palace grounds directly in front of the Royal Palace in Madrid, Spain. We had just completed a guided tour inside the palace.

Our designated photographer, who always carried with him a lightweight tripod, set up his camera on the tripod, peered through the lens to find the perfect focus for our group picture and got ready to switch on the timer.

A young palace guard strode to where we were. He pointed at the tripod, wagged his forefinger at us while exclaiming, "No, no, no. No tripod."

"No tripod? Can't we take pictures?" We asked in unison.

"No tripod. Yes, you can take pictures, but no tripod."

We meekly obeyed. But why, in heaven's name, is that so? What difference can a tripod make?

Lesson learned: *"Sometimes in life we need to ask, 'Can someone please explain this to me?'"*

# BROWN ROAD SIGN

The carving on the tree trunk

It is my understanding that in the USA a brown road sign is used to indicate a site or area for recreational or cultural interest which is open to the public. I believe it stands for the same thing in Canada. In the U.K. it indicates a tourist attraction.

About 18 years ago, we were driving on a highway in Spain. We were on our way to Madrid via Seville. It was kind of a lazy drive. Although we found pleasure in watching the passing scenery and landscape, we were a bit bored. Then suddenly we got excited when we saw a brown sign. We knew an interesting area would be coming up soon. We could all take a break, stretch out our legs and perhaps see something remarkable.

The brown sign said something about a "Castillo", a castle. The rest of the sign, we couldn't understand. Aha, it must be a castle turned into a museum! We followed the sign, exited the highway and drove through a tree-lined street. One tree stood out among the others. At its trunk (mind you, this is a live tree) was a life size carving of a person.

Our interest grew when we saw a grand edifice at the end of the road. Since there was no parking area, we stopped at one side of the circular driveway. There was no one around. We loved it. That way we could get unobstructed pictures of the place and of ourselves.

The gate to the castle itself was open. But there was not a soul in sight. We knocked at the gate. A young woman dressed in the typical European housemaid attire with apron and cap came out. Using the very limited Spanish that Leo knew, we told her that we were tourists and that we would love to go inside. We learned that it was "privado", a private residence ... at least, that's what she seemed to say. She was willing to let us into the foyer, though.

If, indeed, that was a private residence, we declined her invitation for fear of getting her in trouble. We told her we will just take pictures at the rotunda in front of the castle.

As we got busy having our "Kodak moments" a sophisticated looking man in an elegant car arrived. He eyed us in an indignant and disgusting manner, but did not say a word. He must have thought, "Who are these trespassers?"

But of course we did not know ... and up to now we still don't know ... if we trespassed into some Spanish nobleman's private property or if he, too, just happened to be there.

It was a brown sign that led us there!

Lesson learned: *"Colors can deceive. ... Did it?"*

# ONE BLURRY PICTURE

Monasterio de El Escorial

Our trip to Spain was really an adventure, exactly how we wanted it to be. We rented a car, drove ourselves from one city or town to another and agreed to sleep wherever darkness caught up with us. It was the mid-1990s and the GPS was still unheard of.

We were in Madrid the whole day, but sleep will have to wait outside the city. We were hoping to find an inexpensive hotel out there.

Our worn out map indicated that the Monasterio de San Lorenzo de El Escorial is about 30 miles northwest of Madrid in the foothills of Sierra de Guadarrama. We headed in that direction. Tired and sleepy, we checked in at the first hotel we found. At the hotel lobby we picked up a copy of a brochure about El Escorial. It presented a massive edifice and lots of very interesting historical information.

The complex consisted of a Monastery, a Royal Palace, and a Mausoleum for the interment of the Spanish Monarchy starting with Charles I and Isabella II of Portugal. This location was personally chosen by King Philip II. Here he built an imposing structure to commemorate Spain's victory over King Henry II of France in the battle of San Quentin on August 10, 1557, the feast day of St. Lawrence.

The gates had barely opened when we reached El Escorial very early the next morning. We knew we had a long day ahead of us. We toured this colossal (14.9 miles of corridors) complex. The palace itself was very simple, but the Monastery was extremely impressive. One special feature that I recall was a concealed window at level with the main altar of the basilica. We were told that this was specially designed so that King Philip II, in his later years when he suffered from gout, could attend Holy Mass without leaving his bed.

We walked down a few marble steps to the crypt called the Pantheon de los Reyes where the coffins of almost all the monarchs of Spain were to be found. The entrance to the crypt was spectacular, as was the gilded roof of the pantheon. The pantheon walls were made of marble ornamented with gold plated bronze. They were magnificent! A place truly fit for a king! Here the remains of the Bourbons and the Habsburgs lie in state, starting with the Roman Emperor Charles V who ruled Spain as Charles I, Kings Philip II, III, IV, Kings Charles II, III,IV, Louis I, Ferdinand IV and VII, Alfonso XII and XIII, and some relatives.

The center of my attention was the tomb of King Philip II, the monarch after whom my homeland, the Philippines, was named. After having found it, I asked my sister to take a picture ... just one picture. She instructed me to stand beside King Philip's tomb. Then she carefully focused and framed the photograph to be sure that I was on the side with the tomb clearly visible to my left. Remember that this was long before digital cameras when each shot had to be perfect so as to not waste any of our precious but limited film.

During the entire trip we used up 12 rolls of film with 24 frames per roll, giving us 288 pictures altogether.

The blurry picture

As soon as we returned home, I had all 12 rolls developed and printed. Two hundred eighty-seven pictures were beautiful, sharp, and clear. That one single shot ... that precious shot ... of my king and I ... came out blurry. It was a different kind of blur. It looked like light was streaming across the whole room, not in a beam, but scattered to cause a topsy-turvy kind of blur. That was spooky! I felt a tingling sensation run down my spine when I first saw that picture.

Was King Philip II camera shy? We will never know. Or was it simply a coincidence? Perhaps my sister got excited, so much so that her hands were not steady enough? But one out of 288 pictures ... that's quite beyond me.

Do I believe in ghosts? Hmmmmm, let me reflect upon that!

Lesson learned: *"The significance of 'One' should never be underrated."*

❧❧

## AN UNEXPECTED POLICE ESCORT IN BARCELONA

It was 5:30 a.m., Barcelona, Spain. We were on our way to the airport for our flight back to the USA. Although we had studied the city map, we couldn't find our way out of the city to the highway that leads to the airport. Our limited knowledge of Spanish was clearly a handicap. The absence of pedestrians at such an early hour was another problem. There was no one to ask for directions.

We hit a red light. Luck was with us. A police car with a couple of police officers stopped beside our car. Leo rolled down the driver's side window. So did Elena behind him. This she did to show our alien-looking faces.

"Senor, aeropuerto?" That was Leo with a couple of Spanish words. From the passenger side where I was seated I waved the map to catch the officer's attention. He understood.

The light was still red. The officer who was on the passenger side exited the police car. He tried to give us directions in halting English.

The light turned green. He knew that we didn't get it. He told us to pull over as he climbed back into his car in order to park in front of us. He came out of the car again, asked for my map and motioned for Leo to get out so that he could assist us. Using the hood as a desk, he spread out the map and both men studied it. The second officer joined them. From where I was seated I could glean from their body language that there was a problem.

Eventually, the officers folded the map, gave it back to Leo and said. "Follow us. We take you to highway. We blink our lights, you go straight to aeropuerto."

"Thank you. Muchos gracias, Senores."

They smiled, jumped back into their car and drove slowly in front of us.

We followed them for about ten minutes. Then we saw their lights blinking as they waved and turned right, exiting the highway.

We waved back and drove straight ahead to the airport.

Lesson learned: *"Where there is kindness, the world becomes a better place."*

# SIESTA TIME IN PORTUGAL

For tourists like us who want to make the most of our time in any place we visit and who plan to see and experience a great deal within a short period of time, we schedule our flights so that we arrive at our destinations at the earliest possible time of the day.

Thus it was when we flew from Newark International Airport in New Jersey to Lisbon, Portugal. We arrived in Lisbon just before noon. We quickly picked up our rental car and drove to the city center to buy supplies for our five-day tour. We needed water and groceries. We excitedly anticipated at least a five-hour tour of the sights of the Old Town after we had made our purchases and before we drove off to our next destination.

It was a few minutes past twelve noon when we arrived at the city center. The city was deserted. Nothing was stirring. The shops were closed. Traffic was exceptionally light. Our excitement changed to wonder. Where are all the people? Why are all the business establishments closed? Why is the traffic so light? There was no one to inquire from.

The silence was broken by the clickety-clickety-clack of a pair of high heels. We turned around and saw a young woman in a business suit. We spoke to her. Our wonder changed to disappointment. "It is siesta time. The city is on its mid-day rest. Businesses will reopen after an hour."

We went back to our car, sat down like local persons would, and painfully let the time go by.

Lesson learned: *"When in Portugal do as the Portuguese do. Take your time!"*

# THE BEDSPREADS OF ALJUSTREL

One of the most well known pilgrimage sites for Catholics all over the world is Fatima in Portugal. Siblings Francisco and Jacinta Marto, who were from Aljustrel, together with their cousin Lucia dos Santos, who was from Valinhos, have witnessed apparitions of an angel in 1916 and several apparitions of the Blessed Virgin Mary in 1917. These miracles have been recognized by the Catholic church as authentic.

We visited Fatima in 1996. Since our trip was an unguided tour, we used local maps to get to our destinations. Aljustrel is a tiny village which triggered our interest because it was the birthplace of the Marto children. We learned that their original house, which was still there, had been converted to a shrine and was open to visitors. We drove over a few miles of dust roads in Portugal's rural areas to reach Aljustrel.

As we approached the village we saw a modest souvenir store. Souvenir-crazy people that we are, we jumped out of our car. The bedspreads for which Portugal is famous were beautiful. There were so many choices available. It took us some time to decide which to buy. Finally we made our selections, paid, and jumped back into the car.

Leo was about to start the car. "Hey, listen! What did we come here for? To buy the bedspreads or to visit the Marto residence?"

This brought us back to our senses. Elena returned to the store to ask for directions. It turned out that the simple old pitiful-looking shack adjacent to the store was the holy place which we were here to visit.

We entered the house. We were met by one of the children's

cousins who showed us the little room where the children were born and died. This visit evoked mixed feelings from us. We saw how poor and downtrodden the family was in the eyes of humanity, but how richly blessed they were in the eyes of God.

We said a little prayer and left. As we drove off we felt guilt and shame for focusing more on souvenirs rather than on what really mattered. Being in the simple abode of the holy children who were blessed in a very special way by God through a direct contact with the Blessed Virgin Mary should have been our major concern.

Lesson learned: *Quote from the Little Prince: "What is essential is invisible to the eye."*

# BRATWURST

The Shrine of the Black Madonna

Bel, Leo, Ehrie, and I arrived at Einsiedeln, Switzerland to pay a visit to the Shrine of the Black Madonna which dates back to the year 829. It was early December and the streets have been turned into a Christmas market.

We were immediately drawn into the spirit of the season as we inched our way to the shrine. Before we could get there, we smelled the inviting aroma of bratwurst coming from one of the stands. We joined the queue for a meal of that famous sausage pinched in a bread roll. A bottle of soda completed the meal. We got hooked on bratwurst. It was so delicious!

We then proceeded to the shrine. We were amazed at the beauty of the grandiose facade of this ancient church. But that was nothing compared to the exquisite adornments in the church's interior. I was dumbstruck with what I saw. For some time we simply stood there admiring the church's display of awe inspiring religious art. Then we knelt down to pray.

The square outside the shrine was lined with stores selling a multitude of religious gift items. We spent a lot of time browsing over the displayed objects, bought a few souvenirs, then walked back to the Christmas market, and explored other places nearby.

Before long we felt famished. We looked for a restaurant that serves bratwurst. We had decided that we will have bratwurst for lunch, but that we preferred eating while seated in a restaurant so as to give rest to our aching feet. We entered two restaurants but couldn't find bratwurst on the menu.

Finally we spoke to a waiter and told him that, "All we want to eat is bratwurst in a bread roll." We were like carnivorous teenagers longing for bratwurst at any cost.

"I understand. I'm sorry we don't serve that here. You have to go back to the street market. The food you're looking for can be bought only at stands from street vendors."

So back to the street vendors we marched, found and bought what we wanted, and ate it with gusto while sitting at the street curb.

Ahhhh, bratwurst!!! You're worth sitting down for at the curb!

Interior of the Shrine of the Black Madonna

Lesson learned: *"One usually finds the right thing if one looks for it in the right place."*

# THE ALPS AND THE CATARACT

The above picture shows Bel and I at the exact spot where I discovered my cataract. Note the glistening Alps in the background.

In 2001 we took the train from Lucerne to Engelberg on our way to the 10,000 foot high Mt. Titlis which is one of the most fascinating winter resorts in Switzerland. While waiting at the Titlis base station for the revolving aerial cable car ride to the panoramic peak, I was enthralled by the view surrounding me. The sun's rays were striking the alps. The brightness of the shimmering white mountain tops caused the awesome rays of the sun to bounce back towards me. I stopped in my tracks and photographed the magnificent view.

During that time, digital cameras were not yet a common commodity. To take a picture I had to shut one eye, place the viewfinder over the other eye, then click. I shut my right eye and took the view as seen by my left eye. It was an incredible picture-perfect view.

For some reason which I cannot explain, after putting the camera back in its case, I placed my left hand over my left eye and I observed the same view with my right eye. I was shocked. The view was completely different. Everything was blurry. I blinked several times, gave my eyes some rest, then I repeated the process. I continued to see the same blurry view.

Back in New Jersey, despite my phobia for doctor's visits, I immediately made an appointment with a famous ophthalmologist, Dr. John R. Stabile. He gave me a thorough eye examination after which he informed me that I had a problematic cataract in my right eye. I had a choice between retaining that problem or undergoing appropriate surgery so as to see the world more clearly. I chose the logical second option.

Viewing the world through blurry lenses, either of the eye or of the mind, we lose the clarity and the sharpness of vision. And surely we miss a lot of the beauty surrounding us.

Until now, many years after that incident, I cannot but wonder why it had to be the dazzling beauty of the Swiss Alps which made me discover the cataract in my right eye. I am assuredly most grateful.

Lesson learned: *"Travel unravels unexpected issues."*

# SWISS WATCHES AGAINST HUNGER

Geneva viewed from atop
St. Peter's Cathedral

It was past noon. We were walking the streets of Geneva, Switzerland looking for a decent but inexpensive place for lunch. We met a Filipina. We stopped and asked for her advice. She gave us a name and directed us to a place a few blocks away. "Be sure to go to the second floor. That's where you'll find the food court."

"*Salamat.* Thank you." Our pace quickened. We were starving.

We found the place. Upon entering the building we noticed that the ground floor had a huge display of reasonably priced Swiss watches. They were elegant looking but unexpectedly inexpensive.

Carrying a bag full of Swiss watches
on the streets of Geneva

We started browsing around from one showcase to another. The saleslady brought some watches out for our closer scrutiny. She took out more ... and more ... and more. Excitedly, we chose and put aside one, then two, then ... . It went on for about an hour.

In the end, Bel has picked out one pricey piece and several inexpensive ones; Ehrie selected four; Leo chose five and I selected five.

As we were paying for our "loot", we remembered that we have forgotten what we were there for. We were hungry for food ... but not really ... not anymore.

We proceeded to the second floor. The sweet aroma of food brought our hunger back.

Lesson learned: *"Is hunger just a state of mind?"*

# IT'S GREAT TO BE BILINGUAL

November 2001. The fearless four: Bel, Ehrie, Leo, and I, despite the still gnawing fears of 9/11, flew to Switzerland for a week-long vacation. Our itinerary included Zurich, Geneva, Luzern, Einseideln, then back to Zurich for our flight back home.

Surprisingly the flights to and from Zurich were full. On our return flight Bel and I were seated beside a pleasant middle-aged lady. During the earlier part of the flight Bel and I were busy chatting in *Tagalog,* our Philippine national language. We were excitedly recalling the events of our recent trip and were both looking forward to traveling to another interesting destination.

Meal was served. This interrupted our chatter. The lady said something funny about the food. That broke the ice. We caught her comment, so we all laughed.

That started a conversation among the three of us. We spoke about the meal, then the weather, then Switzerland. Finally I popped a question. "Are you visiting the U.S., or are you coming home?" I asked. She said, "I'm a resident. How about you, where are you from?"

"The U.S.A. ... We're American citizens," Bel and I proudly responded.

"So you are Americans. But your conversation didn't sound anything like you're from the U.S.A.," she commented.

"Oh, you mean our language," I responded. "That's the advantage of being bilingual."


Lesson learned: *"After English, learn to speak a second language!"*

# HOW YOU SAY IT DOES MATTER

The Eiffel Tower

It was early morning in Paris. Elena, Connie, Leo, and I decided that our first destination for the day was the Eiffel Tower. Newbies that we all were, we had difficulty in finding which subway train to take. Not one of us knew how to speak French. Anyway, I had the courage to ask a man who looked like a local resident.

"Sir, we would like to go see the Eiffel Tower. Which train do we take?"

"Quoi?" I thought I heard, "What?" Fine. I repeated my question. I got the same answer. Then I understood that he did not understand. So with my two hands, I swiped the shape of the Eiffel tower in the air. The sign language worked. We saw a broad smile on his face as he said, "Ahhhhhh, Tour Eiffel!", pronouncing the name "toor eeeeeefel". With more signs and gestures we finally got the correct directions.

"Merci, Monsieur Eeeeeefel."

Lesson learned: *"Know the local language ... if at all possible. Otherwise, improvise."*

# DINNER AT LOURDES

Basilica of the Immaculate
Conception, Lourdes, France

Most of our travels take place during the so-called "low" season for obvious reasons: we travel more for less and there are no lines to queue up for, nor are there a throng of pilgrims to squeeze your way through.

Thus, when we arrived in Lourdes, France after a long drive from Paris, we were so pleased that the town, the shops, the shrine, the basilica, and the grotto were all practically empty. It was early March 1995, a good time to visit, to pray without distraction, to get very close to the miraculous spring, and to touch the grotto where the Blessed Mother appeared to Bernadette Soubirous in 1858. As Catholics we were deeply moved by the powerful impact of this extremely spiritual environment. The short time we spent here at the Basilica of the Immaculate Conception enabled us to truly capture the essence of this holy setting.

We parked our car in front of a souvenir shop at the edge of town, very close to the entrance to the shrine. It was about 5:30 in the afternoon. There were no shoppers. We entered the gift shop and asked the owner if it was okay to park our car almost at her door. We asked her what time she closes. Her answer was a very kind "We will wait for you."

    We walked up to the massive basilica to pray. There was a

handful of people inside. Then we walked down to the grotto, sat down on the open air prayer seats, walked beside and around the glass-protected spring; then we approached the altar. We had the whole area to ourselves: Connie, Leo, Elena, and I. We stayed for some time meditating, praying, and looking around. The sun was almost setting when we realized that not one of us had thought of bringing along a water container for the holy water from the spring. Leo ran quickly to the gift shop where he bought a dozen small plastic containers in the shape of Our Lady of Lourdes.

Having filled up our containers, we walked back to the gift shop which the owner kept open for the four of us. We were in the midst of shopping when Leo suddenly remembered that we hadn't booked a hotel and we didn't know where to go for dinner. He left us to continue shopping. Meanwhile, he ran the errands.

He was back in a very short while. "Mission accomplished", he said. "Ladies, I checked in at the hotel next door. The best news is that there is a McDonald's down this street."

The storekeeper heard this and said with emphasis, "McDonald's? Why McDonald's? No, no, no."

What we wanted to tell her, but did not, was that we were penny-pinching.

"No, not McDonald's", she continued. "You must go to our local restaurant. They serve authentic native food. Very delicious. You'll like it. I'll take you there."

Having heard that, we could not refuse. We paid for our purchases. She called an elderly man to mind the store. "I'm taking these Americans to ... (I can't remember the name of the place) ... for dinner.

And so, off we went in two cars. She led the way. The restaurant was exotic. It was ethnic both in ambiance and in its menu. We loved both the place and the food. We got carried away, forgot our penny-pinching, ate to our hearts' content, and swiped our cards after the meal. No regrets for having spent more than we intended to! This meal was a fitting complement to an unforgettable experience.

Lesson learned: *"You may never pass this way again, so make the most of your stay."*

# OF FACT AND FICTION

The "Sound of Music" kept playing in our minds as we set off for our guided tour of Salzburg, Austria. We were to see some of the places where that super famous musical movie was filmed.

At a distance from the highway our guide pointed out to us the cathedral where the wedding took place. Sorry, it was out of the way. We did not have time to go there.

We reached the center of Salzburg.

Remember that scene where the children were singing while riding their bikes? We walked around that area. The strains of "Do, re, mi" ... seemed so real.

Remember the cemetery where the family hid from the pursuing SS guards? It looked so big in the movie. Truth is, it is a small cemetery. Our guide pointed out to us the headstones which appeared in the movie.

"But where is the palatial residence where the von Trapp family lived? We want to see it."

"That my friends, was just a movie set."

Lesson learned: *"Separate fact from fiction."*

# THIS PEST IS NOT A MENACE

The Chain Bridge

Our visit to Budapest, Hungary in 2002, started with a train ride from Vienna, Austria. The experience was a mix of the drab and the interesting. We left Vienna with the lively strains of Mozart's music still hanging over our minds. Immediately after we crossed the border there was a sudden change in the landscape from that of vibrant Vienna to the dull, almost lifeless Hungary.

There was, however, a redeeming quality to the otherwise dreary entry to Hungary. Both the Austrian and Hungarian governments offered services that made travel for tourists between the two countries very convenient. As soon as we crossed the border an Austrian Immigration Officer walked through the train compartments to mark our passports with the exit stamp. Right behind him was a Hungarian Immigration Officer who marked our passports with the entry stamp. The two officers were followed by a Tourist Information agent who gave us all the information needed for a pleasant stay in Hungary. He even exchanged some of our dollars to the Hungarian currency, Forinth. These services were excellent. It saved a lot of time that we would have spent if we had to endure these bureaucratic red tapes by ourselves.

Upon reaching Budapest, we went straight to our hotel which was conveniently located at the center of the city. We ate a quick lunch, picked up a brochure at the hotel lobby, then started right away on our self-guided walking tour.

It was while reading the brochure that we learned some surprising details about the city we were set to explore.

Budapest is the capital of Hungary; a city situated along the banks of the Danube river. ... That we already knew.

The name "Budapest" came about in 1873 when the towns of Buda and Obuda on the Danube's right bank, and the town of Pest on the river's left bank were merged. ... This we did not know. Although we heard about this earlier, we thought it was a big joke. ... Now we know that Budapest is really Buda and Pest.

Buda consisted of the hills where government buildings, palaces, and villas are located. Pest is the flat area where the commercial and industrial sections are concentrated.

We learned that our hotel was in Pest. This is where we savored the famous Hungarian desserts. We ate at one of the most highly recommended confectioner shops. Without fully understanding the menu, we decided to order a variety of them and shared the food among us. Everything was either so creamy or richly chocolate ... ah, simply delicious! Pest, after all, is anything but a pest!

After the treat we walked across the beautiful and elegant Chain Bridge which spans over the Danube, not only to join Pest to Buda, but to transport us from the new part of the city to the old section where the palaces and villas were located. Here we toured the Old Town, particularly the Fisherman's Bastion and the Royal Palace. From up on the hills of Buda our eyes feasted on the panoramic view of the Danube below. It was then that we began to appreciate the beauty of the alluring city of Budapest. We stayed for a few more days exploring the numerous fascinating tourist areas both in Buda and in Pest.

Lesson learned: *"What's in a name???? Not much ... sometimes!"*

# DINING IN THE MOUNTAINS OF BUDAPEST

As part of the package tour we bought for Hungary, there was to be a folklore show and dinner at Urbadhaz, on the Buda side of Budapest. The restaurant is described as an upscale tourist attraction overlooking the city of Budapest. The tour company informed us that this was not part of the guided tour. However, there would be no problem since we could easily take a taxi from the hotel.

The dinner was scheduled for 7:00 p.m. Elena, Racquel, Bel and myself, with the help of the hotel staff who directed the driver where to take us, excitedly boarded the taxi.

After a few minutes drive we noticed that we were driving away from the city onto a deserted winding road. We were going high up in the mountains through an uninhabited forest-like area. It was getting dark. There were no street lights. There were no houses. In fact there were no signs of human existence along the way.

Wild panicky thoughts ran through our minds. Four women in a strange place with a strange man who doesn't know a single word of English except, perhaps "Yes" or "No".

"Where is this driver taking us? This road seems to lead to nowhere." We softly murmured to each other in our dialect.

There was nothing we could do but pray ... and pray very hard. The silence among the four of us was torturous. The darkness was frightening.

Fifteen more nervous minutes. We finally found ourselves on top of a mountain on which was nestled an attractive restaurant overlooking the brightly lit city below. "Thank God, we are safe," we happily whispered to each other.

"Look," I exclaimed. "Even the stars have come down from the heavens and settled down below us! What a spectacle!"

With all our fears gone, we relished every moment of our evening. The ambiance, the food, the service, the show ... all of these more than made up for the jittery feelings we had on the way up.

*Lesson learned: "Trust in the higher power!"*

# ATTENTION!!! ACHTUNG!!!

In 1791 Friedrich Wilhelm II commissioned the Bradenburg Gate. It was the entrance to "Unter den Linden", the boulevard which led to the palace of the monarchs. The gate became the national symbol of Germany. During the Cold War it was part of the infamous and symbolic Berlin Wall which separated East Berlin from West Berlin.

When the Berlin Wall fell in 1989, the Brandenburg Gate reopened. It became the symbol of a new reunified Germany, and since then has been one of the most visited landmarks in that country.

We were at the Brandenburg Gate. Personally I was having mixed emotions as I walked though the gate. I felt a great sadness for those who were kept prisoners in the East. Yet this day brought me immense happiness as I experienced the freedom of crossing the gate thus proving to myself that it was open to signify more than just a unified Berlin. It is a monument to the fall of Communism.

We alighted from our bus in what was previously the Eastern sector, passed through the gate's wide open archway to what used to be the Western sector. Hundreds of tourists like us were busy taking pictures of the gate as well as with the gate. I was wandering by myself around the area when I saw a young man in full military uniform standing at attention and as immobile as a statue near one of the smaller archways. I thought he was some kind of an honor guard. So I called my daughter and signaled for her to snap a photo of him and me while I sneaked up beside him.

I was about to leave when he suddenly moved and said to me, "Ma'am, would a dollar be fine with you?"

"But of course," I replied, trying to hide my embarrassment for acting like a sneak. I took a dollar bill from my purse and handed it to him. He was pleased and thanked me for it.

I took a closer look at his uniform. It was the uniform of the East German Communist soldier. He was there to pose with visitors and get compensated for his stern face and snappy salute.

Lesson learned: *"Things aren't always what they seem."*

## THE GREEN VAULT OF DRESDEN

The Parade of the Nobles

Our tour of Germany brought us to Berlin, Meisen, Dresden and Potsdam.

Going to Dresden, we drove beside the Elbe River. Dresden, also known as Florence on the Elbe, is the capital of Saxony. This city was severely damaged by bombs during WWII. But today, it has been brought back to its past glory. And what a glorious sight it is! Almost clustered together in the center of the old city are the Church of Our Lady (Protestant), the Catholic Cathedral (the biggest church in Saxony) with its 3000-pipe organ, the Palace of Culture, the Royal Palace, the Parade of the Nobles (a mural made of porcelain tiles manufactured in Meissen depicting the 35 members of the Saxon royalty), the Old Masters Gallery and The Green Vault Museum, each magnificent in its own right.

After having guided us through the entire area, our guide Monika gave us an hour of free time during which we could browse wherever we chose. She emphatically recommended a visit to The Green Vault Museum.

"What kind of museum is it? I mean, what do we find in there?" I asked.

"It is a museum of jewelry. I promise you, it is beautiful in there."

What I had in mind was something like the Crown Jewels of England. Having seen the jewelry displayed in London, in Istanbul and in the Smithsonian in Washington D.C., I almost did not want to waste my time. But she insisted that we see it, and thank goodness, we did. Because on display there, were not jewels that one wears on one's body, but masterpieces of jewelry like I have never seen before, and perhaps will never see anywhere else. These are displays of intricate kingly treasures and gifts from one kingdom to another. The most magnificent display is the miniature model of the court of an Indian king which consisted of more than 130 golden figures which dazzled incredibly with thousands of diamond stones.

Among the countless exhibits were numerous precious objects made of gold, silver, ivory, ebony, jasper, amber, bronze, and other materials adorned with diamonds, rubies, pearls, and other priceless gems.

Sadly, photography was not permitted.

Everything in that remarkable museum was a precious work of art of such quality and variety that probably will not be seen in other jewelry museums.

Lesson learned: *"When you think you have already seen it all, think again for you can never be sure!"*

# THE ASHES OF POMPEII

A postcard from Pompeii

It was mid-afternoon when we reached Pompeii from Rome. It was planned to be a short trip, a quick visit to the ruins of Pompeii. Mt. Vesuvius loomed majestically five miles yonder.

Pompeii was an ancient city, flourishing under Roman rule since 200 B.C. until one day in 79 A.D., Mt. Vesuvius unleashed its earth-shaking fury. It blew its top and covered the whole city and its 20,000 inhabitants in ashes.

After Pompeii was buried it was lost to history until 1631 when the volcano erupted again, killing 4,000 people. During the restoration work after the second eruption, the workers discovered the ruins of the city which had been forgotten for 1600 years. It took another three hundred years before the excavations were sufficiently extensive to reveal the city beneath the ashes.

This is what we were there to see!

The main gate to the excavation area was half-closed when we approached it. We asked the guard if we could still enter.

"Sorry, but you just missed the last group of tourists. We are closing in ten minutes."

We pleaded, begged, almost in tears, but his "No" was as firm as the mummified bodies within.

The tourist area is surrounded by wrought iron bars. Although you can peer through, not much can be seen from the outside.

Undaunted, Arsol and I kept walking alongside the fence. To our great surprise we reached a wide open gate. This must have been the back door. Hesitantly, we walked in. It was like we would take four steps in, then two steps out. We acted like two kids trying to sneak in.

But the fear of being caught as trespassers was in our minds. "And what if they close the gate behind us?"

A man was busy fixing his jeep just behind the gate. He saw us. I could sense that he was laughing at our childish behavior. He stopped what he was doing and approached us. "Would you like to come in?" His perfect English startled us.

"Yes, very much so. But the guard at the ticket booth told us that we were late and that he was ready to close. We feel very sad because we traveled all the way from the Philippines to see Pompeii and we just missed it."

"Come in. I'll show you around."

"Are you sure we can do that?"

"Positive! Let's go."

Arsol and I sounded like excited children. We were practically jumping with joy! The kind gentleman whose name I cannot recall led us in, guided us through the ruins and showed us the mummified bodies of some of the thousands who were buried in ashes. He also explained many items of interest to us. He would have guided us farther into the excavated city but it was getting late and we had to leave.

*"Grazie! Grazie multi!"* That was so kind and gracious of him.

We left Pompeii, not only with remembrances of what we saw, but also with a celebration of a stranger's kindness.

Lesson learned: *"When a door closes in on you, go find another one."*

# THE MONKS OF ASSISI

A pose with the kind Monks of Assisi

Except for two gentlemen and a group of monks in their conspicuous brown habits, the train compartment we traveled in from Rome to Assisi was nearly empty.

When the train stopped at the Assisi station, Arsol and I were perturbed to find out that the town proper was not within walking distance. We wondered aloud how we could get there.

One gentleman, after noticing that we looked dazed and lost, came to our rescue. He spoke fluent English. He told us that we needed to take a bus to the city, but that we had to purchase the tickets before the bus arrives. He led us to the ticket booth. We learned that he was taking the same bus.

We waited.

Meanwhile the monks were busy boarding a van which came to fetch them. When they drove by us they momentarily stopped and one of them called out, "Father, we've got room in here. Come with us."

"So, he is a priest. No wonder he has a compassion for lost souls." I whispered to Arsol.

The friendly and kind priest waved them on and motioned to them that he was coming with us. *"Turista,"* he told them.

The monks drove off.

A few seconds later, we saw the van making a U-turn. It stopped in front of us. One monk, the only one conversant in English (so they told us later), stepped out of the van and told us that they made room for the three of us.

"Where are you headed for?" asked the English-speaking

monk.

"Nowhere in particular but to see the city," we replied. For some reason, still unknown to me until now, we did not tell them that we were in fact headed for the Basilica of St. Francis of Assisi.

"Okay then. We will let you off at the center of the city. It's a small city, so you won't get lost. Is that fine with you?"

"That would be great, Brother. Thank you so much for your kindness."

"Ladies, the last bus to the train station leaves at 5:00 p.m. The bus stops there. Don't be late." That was the priest pointing out the bus stop and giving us his fatherly instructions before we left the van.

"Yes, Father. And thank you very much."

"*Grazie!*" We called out as we waved them goodbye and as the van-load of monks waved back to us.

Arsol and I toured the quaint old city on foot, stopping here and there at the shops. We visited the Shrine of Saint Clare. It was closed. We walked towards the main objective of our trip there: the Basilica of St. Francis of Assisi. When we reached the top of the hill where the church was located, guess who welcomed us? The monks who gave us a ride!

"*Buongiorno! Benvenuto!*" We felt like old friends seeing each other again after a long time. We posed for pictures with them.

Our visit to the shrine took place a few months after the devastating earthquake that shook the city and destroyed numerous buildings including part of the basilica. Hence, the basilica was closed to visitors. Construction materials cluttered the yard.

We begged our new found friends to allow us to just take a peek inside.

"Permission granted ... but only a peek for two minutes. Don't get inside. Anything may crumble down on you at any time."

We entered the side entrance to the lower level, took a quick peek and saw the destruction within. We did not have the chance to appreciate the well known frescoes, statues, chapels and paintings.

The monks were watching carefully and reminded us it was time to get out to safe grounds. We did.

"*Grazie,* Brothers. You have been so kind to us."

"Arrivederci, Assisi! I hope to come back some time in the not too distant future."

The Basilica of St. Francis

Lesson learned: *"Let us joyfully celebrate the kindness of strangers."*

# SHOES ARE OFF LIMITS HERE

The Blue Mosque

In Istanbul, Turkey we went visiting some tourist attraction sites by ourselves. From a distance we saw the six towering minarets and the imposing structures that make up the Blue Mosque. We walked towards it. It was open, so we went inside.

Excited as I always am when in a new place, I rushed through the open door towards the richly decorated pulpit or minber. An old man saw me. He motioned for me to go back to the door. I was astonished. But I knew why when I saw my companions taking off their shoes and leaving them at the door.

It is interesting to note that during the Muslim prayer time, the hundreds or thousands that come into the mosque leave their footwear at the door, then enter barefoot or in their socks. Despite the large number of pairs of footwear, I assume everyone goes home with their own pair. ... or don't they? I wonder.

I wish tourists, on the other hand, would have been instructed to bring a plastic bag where they can place their shoes and carry them in.

Even after returning to the U.S.A. my curiosity had not lessened. I asked a Muslim acquaintance to explain the reason behind the practice. "There are three reasons," she said. "One, is respect for a holy place; two, for hygienic reasons; and three, historically, most footwear were made of dead animals' skins. This material is not allowed in the mosque."

So, there we go! Another lesson learned by me.

Lesson learned: *"Another culture, other rules to obey."*

# IGNORANCE IS BLISS

Snow in Cappadocia

During the early years of my international travels, one of our least concerns was the weather at our destination. In fact, we never bothered to check the weather data before booking our trip. Looking back, this was a stupid mistake. Somehow, we managed to go on despite this "sin of omission".

Cappadocia, Turkey is not the best place to visit in early February. We were unaware of this. Because of our ignorance we never factored in the possibility of unfavorable climate conditions when we made our travel plans.

That Friday, Istanbul was bright, warm, and sunny. A local travel agent booked us for a Saturday afternoon flight to Kayseri. We were to be met at the airport by Sami who was to drive us through Nevsehir to Nar for an overnight stay at the modern Peri Tower Hotel. On the following day we would tour the area, after which we were scheduled to fly back to Istanbul in the evening.

The Turkish Airlines flight to Kayseri was quick and smooth. As expected, Sami met us at the airport and whisked us on an uneventful two-hour drive to the hotel. Ali, a very pleasant and friendly young man, joined us for dinner at the hotel. He was to be our guide for tomorrow's tour. Before he left, he reminded us that pickup time will be exactly 9:00 a.m. "There are so many exciting places to visit. So let's start on time."

I awoke at 7:00 a.m., eagerly looking forward to another wonderful and pleasurable journey to several destinations. I pulled the drapes open to welcome the sun and to wake my sister who was still sleeping soundly. I was shocked to see large snowflakes coming down from the sky. As far as my eyes could see, the earth was white with snow.

"Oh, Lord," I gasped. "Our tour is doomed. This is completely unexpected. Istanbul was sunny when we left. The weather was equally fine when we arrived here."

"What are you complaining about at this early hour?" My sister murmured as she stirred on the bed.

"Wake up. Look outside the window. We're doomed. We may not be able to leave this hotel, much less fly back to Istanbul tonight."

She jumped out of bed, saw the snow that was falling like crazy and looked down at the all-white surroundings below.

Nevertheless, we dressed up. We went to the dining room to enjoy our continental breakfast. "If we can't go out, at least we have enjoyed the food." That was Leo's way of making the most of whatever the day had in store for us.

At a quarter of nine we were in the lobby waiting for Ali, partly expecting to hear from him apologies about the nasty weather and the cancellation of our tour, but partly hoping that we would proceed despite the odds.

At exactly 9:00 a.m., a smiling Ali appeared at the main door. He was not a wee bit bothered by the pouring snow. "Let's go!"

"Let's go? How can we? ... In this snow?" There was disbelief in my voice.

Yes, we are going. Don't worry. The chains have been securely fastened to the tires of our snowmobile. Plus, our first stop will be the Underground City at Kaymakli. I assure you, there won't be any trace of snow in there."

So, off we sailed through the snow-covered streets of Cappadocia. The Underground City consisted of a four-story maze of excavations consisting of adequately ventilated underground homes, wine tanks, water systems, wells, churches, baptismal stones, animal shelters, cemeteries, food storage, exit tunnels, and secret escape passages.

Four more stories are waiting to be excavated below. What makes this building truly incredible is that it is both complex and simple. For what can be more simple yet complex than to have such a huge structure which can accommodate 5000 people, to be constructed with not a single nut or bolt, screw, nail, or any strucural reinforcement? It is a marvel to the architects and engineers of today.

As we emerged from the hole in the ground to be back on the earth's surface, the snow had stopped falling. The sun was peeking through the clouds. Thanks to our ignorance about the local weather, we were not deterred from coming here at this time of the year, thus giving us a most memorable experience, which would have been denied us had we anticipated this unfavorable weather.

Exploring the Underground
City of Kaymakli

Lesson learned: *"Ignorance is bliss!"*

"Travel is fatal to prejudice, bigotry, and narrow-mindedness, and many of our people need it on these accounts. Broad, wholesome, charitable views of men and things cannot be acquired by vegetating in one little corner of the earth all one's lifetime."

Mark Twain

# FOR A PEACEFUL COEXISTENCE

It was the late 1990s. We were in Istanbul, Turkey. Politics and world news were not my forté. I was not knowledgeable about world affairs.

Leo, Elena and I arranged for a one day tour of the city. Since we were there during the low tourist season, our guide noted that our tour will be a private one, that is, we would be by ourselves. So, we will be using a four-door sedan. We were pleased with the arrangement. There would be less hassle.

Early the next morning our guide came with a van instead of a car. A couple was seated in the back seat. "Would it be okay with you if we travel with this couple?" The question was asked but it sounded like it was a done deal.

But of course we did not mind that this couple would be traveling with us. We're all tourists, visitors in a strange land. We enjoy meeting people and learning about them, anyway. "Okay, no problem at all. Let's go."

We got off the van at our first stop. It was at the Topkapi Palace. We introduced ourselves using our first names. They did, too. She was Dana. He was Adel. They were celebrating their wedding anniversary.

"These are American tourists," the driver volunteered as he pointed to us.

"We are from Iran," the husband countered.

"Oh, from Iran!" I excitedly replied. "Before I came to the U.S.A. I was an engineering professor in the Philippines. There were many Iranians enrolled in our university. In fact I had several of them in my class. There was one who stood out among the others. I remember his last name was Esfahani. Perhaps, by some strange coincidence, you know him?"

"Not really," Dana replied. "That is a common Iranian name, you see."

After a brief silence, she asked, "You said you came from the Philippines. But are you American citizens now?"

"Yes, all three of us are."

"Americans and Iranians. We're traveling together, enjoying the same things together ... and ... at peace with each other. Why can't our governments be at peace with each other, too?" she lamented.

"Yes, why not?"

Lesson learned: *"Individual relationships can overcome bureaucratic lunacy."*

❧❧

## BELGIUM IN THE DARK OF NIGHT

Late night arrival with Connie and Elena

It was the mid-1990s. A group of us were on an "expedition mode" of traveling from Luxembourg to Belgium to the Netherlands. We didn't know exactly where we were going. Our only guide was a tiny book borrowed from the local library. It contained the maps and hotels with phone numbers.

It was nearly sunset when we left Luxembourg. We knew there were more miles to be driven before we reach Brussels where we planned to stay for the evening. Before it became too dark to read the fine prints of the book, I wrote on a piece of paper the complete address of the hotel where we were to stay when we get to Brussels. I also wrote down the names of the streets which would take us to our destination. Since the city of Brussels is not that big, we were confident that it would not be a problem to find the place.

We reached the city. The area we were in was dark. We stopped to ask for directions. "Sorry. But I really don't have the slightest idea where this address is located," was the reply we got.

We drove northward; stopped again for directions. We got a similar reply.

We gave ourselves one more chance. We approached a man who was about to start his car. "Surely, he would know." The man read the piece of paper which I handed to him. He, too, shook his head, "Sorry, I don't know the place you're looking for."

"By the way, Sir, is this Brussels?" we asked.

"No, you are 40 kilometers from Brussels. Take this highway and it will bring you to the city."

No wonder we couldn't find the hotel.

It was late at night when we finally reached Brussels. It didn't take us long to find our destination.


Lesson learned:  *"You may never find what you're looking for if you search in the wrong place."*

# DRACULA'S PRACTICAL JOKE ON ME

The Author and her friends with
Bran Castle in the background

Bran Castle or Dracula's Castle stands at the border of Transylvania and Wallachia. Because of a legend written by Bram Stoker in 1897, Bran Castle became more commonly known as Dracula's Castle. Although there is some evidence that Dracula did stay in the castle during his raids into Transylvania, this castle was never owned by him.

In 1377, the Saxons of Brasov built this castle after an edict issued by Louis I of Hungary. The castle was first used in 1378 against the Ottoman Empire. Later it was designated as a taxation post between Transylvania and Wallachia. In 1920 it became the royal residence of Queen Marie; inherited later by her daughter Princess Ileana; seized by the Communist Regime in 1948; then awarded by the Romanian government back to Princess Ileana's son, Prince Dominic of Tuscany who is otherwise known as Dominic Von Habsburg, an architect in New York, who in January 2009 converted the castle into a museum. That, my friends, is Dracula's Castle de-mystified

Upon arriving at the area, we at once knew we had another mountain to climb to get to the castle itself. A huge stone Cross, presumably erected on orders of Queen Marie, greeted the visitor at the base of the fortification. From one of the upper level windows of the castle we had an excellent view of the courtyard and the well. From another window we could see one of the towers across the courtyard and from another window one can just imagine the Queen gazing at all her subjects in the surrounding valley below.

To our utter disappointment, Count Dracula was nowhere to be found. Walking back from the Castle to the town below, we found a spot with a postcard-like view of the castle above. I set my bag down on the grass for a better pose for the camera. When I picked it up, it was four times heavier than before. For a moment I thought it was Count Dracula playing a joke on me. The truth came out soon enough. It was Ronnie, the prankster of our group who, aware that I collect stones from places I visit, had placed a big piece of broken pottery in my bag ... according to him a gift from Count Dracula for my stone collection.

Thanks, Ronnie! It was so generous of you.

Lesson learned: *"While others collect precious stones, I collect priceless ones. They both serve the same purpose: a powerful remembrance of places visited and not forgotten."*

# PICTURES IN SINAIA

Our group picture in front
of Peles Castle

Sinaia, an enchanting city deep in the Carpathian Mountains of Romania, has a special place in my heart. Mariana Buretea, a very close friend of mine who is now deceased, was from this city. She often told me about her good life in the close proximity of Peles Castle. Unfortunately her family's quiet and marvelous life was cruelly interrupted when her country was taken over by the Communists and freedom became for them an idea, but not a reality. It was for this reason that her family immigrated to the United States. For reasons which I may never know now that she is gone, she never told me how beautiful her hometown was. Where she came from is a far cry from the plain sceneries of the New Jersey town where we both lived. Having seen this fairytale-like city, I now fully understand more than ever the pain of loss which she often shared with me. A melancholy tear fell from my eyes for her.

Thus it was with these memories of a dear friend that we visited Peles Castle which was once the residence of the monarchs of Romania. It is now a museum. Our tour group spent some time in that very lovely place in the mountains. Unfortunately we arrived a little late. The palace building itself had just closed. With subtle persuasion from our guide, the guards permitted us into the castle grounds and the open inner courtyard.

We started getting busy with our cameras. We envisioned

the luxurious lifestyle of the monarchs by the elaborate architecture that we saw.

We then stepped out into the huge marble veranda which led to the well kept gardens and then down to the Peles River after which the castle is named.

There was one sculpture that caught my attention. It was a larger than life statue of Queen Elisabeth of Romania reclining in a regal manner. I practically ran towards it to pose for a picture.

Just as I was having my picture taken, one of the guards started flailing his right arm gesturing for me to get out while simultaneously pointing with his left hand at a sign beside the statue. I raised my right hand and gestured back to him something like ... "Leave me alone!"

He continued with his frantic gestures.

In my haste, I accidentally dropped Violy's brand new and expensive digital camera.

At this point, our guide rushed to where we were. He explained to me that the sign meant "Keep off the grass," and that the guard wanted us to step back to the pavement.

I was standing on the grass, alright. I quickly stepped off to the pavement while apologizing to our guide. "Sorry, sorry, but the sign was in Romanian! How could I have possibly understood?"


Lesson learned: *"The difference between languages is a barrier to universal understanding."*

# MIRRORS TO GOSSIP BY

Pulpit inside the
medieval Cathedral

Porvoo, Finland is an idyllic medieval town which looked like time stood still over it. The 13th century cathedral stands sentinel over the picturesque town. The intricately decorated pulpit inside the cathedral standing to the left of the altar reminded us of the days gone by when the celebrant delivered his sermon to the congregation on this elevated lectern. A heavy wooden sculpted side door is also a silent witness to the passage of thousands of men and women who pass through it as they pay homage to God.

Kyrsti, our bubbly guide, made the tour more interesting by telling us colorful stories about past practices and beliefs. This she did as we walked uphill and downhill on the ever changing slopes of the narrow ... very narrow ... cobblestone streets with out-of-the-ordinary names like Ei Talvikunnossapitoa.

"Do you notice anything quite unfamiliar beside the window of that house?" She asked us as we drew near a boldly colored house whose walls touched the edge of the very narrow cobblestone street.

We paused and looked. Then someone from the group said, "Yes, there's a mirror attached to the wall. Is that for passersby who want to check how good they look? Wow, what vanity!"

"You mean, passersby like you? No, it's not for you. Look, it is installed so that you don't really see yourself. It's there so that people inside the house can see you. That way they would know who comes and goes, with whom you come and go, what you do and how you look. It is called a "gossip mirror". As the name implies, it is used by gossips to gossip.

Noticing our incredulity, she added, "It was acceptable then, but not any longer."

See that "Gossip Mirror" at
the side of this house?

Lesson learned: *"Watch out! You are never alone. Someone's watching you!"*

# HEADS IN MOTION

For the many years I have lived on this planet, I knew that one can wordlessly say "Yes" with a nod of the head, and "No" with a shake of the head. In other words, I move my head up and down to say "Yes" and move my head side to side to indicate "No". That was a given. No doubt about that.

Early July 2009, I was on a trip to Bulgaria with ten friends. After a whole day of traveling and visiting various tourist sites we were all hungry and tired. We decided to have dinner at the nearest restaurant. As soon as we were comfortably seated a waitress came to me and asked what drink I wanted.

"A glass of water, please," I replied.

"Do you want ice in your glass of water?" She asked. I nodded affirmatively.

"Do you want a slice of lemon in it?" I shook my head.

Within a couple of minutes, the waitress delivered my glass of water. There was a lovely slice of lemon sitting at the top, but there was no ice. I complained to our guide. She broke into a hearty laugh as she explained, "In Bulgaria, a nod means 'No' and a head shake means 'Yes'. So you got your Bulgarian order, not your American order!"

Lesson learned: *"Be careful with your body language. It could cost you your life!"*

## WHEN THE BLIND LEAD THE BLIND

Entrance to St. Eugenia Church

"Why is Stockholm so sparsely populated?" That was the first question we asked each other during our first day in this capital city of Sweden. We knew the answer when we stopped for lunch at an Asian restaurant where we met a couple of waiters who turned out to be our *kababayans*. They explained to us that during the summer months, the local residents leave the city to either travel to other countries or to vacation at their summer residences in the countryside. As a result, the few people we meet are visitors and tourists like us.

It was Saturday evening. Joy, Sylvia, Marilou, Irene, Bel, Bamba and I ventured out of our hotel in order to dine out, preferably in a local restaurant. Joy volunteered to lead the pack to where she and her friend Mae had lunch earlier. "It's just a few blocks from here." So she thought!

"Aren't we taking the T-Bana?"

"No, we don't need to. It's walking distance from here." Joy assured us.

We walked for 15 minutes ... 25 minutes ... 35 ... 45 ... still no sign of the restaurant!

"Joy, do you know where we're going to? What walking distance are you talking about? We've been walking, yes! But, for heaven's sake, it's too far a distance!"

We never found the place.

Instead we found the All-American restaurant, T.G.I.F.

We would have reluctantly settled for an American meal in Sweden, but the waiting time was two hours. So, we walked again. Finally we found a place to eat. When Bel's order came she found an almost invisible wisp of vegetable on her plate. Whereupon she asked the manager where her veggies are. "Blame it on the French," was his astonishing reply. Although the serving was small, food was good. Truth is, any food would have been good for tired and ravenously hungry people like us.

Across from the restaurant was a park where there was some sort of a prayer rally led by the Salvation Army. After dinner we decided to take a walk in that direction. Irene pointed to a reddish-orange church a few blocks away. "That must be the church where we would attend Sunday Mass tomorrow."

Early the next morning we decided to walk towards the red brick church. But for our group, the rest of Stockholm was still asleep. The streets were practically empty. We were no longer surprised.

We reached the red church. It was closed. And, to our utter disappointment ... we found out that it was not the Catholic Church which we wanted. We needed to find St. Eugenia Church. Irene pulled out the city map from her bag, and with a few other heads, studied it. They turned the map upside-down, then downside-up, looking for the correct orientation. It looked like we were headed in the wrong direction. Just as we were about to make a U-turn, we saw two pedestrians. Sensing that we were lost, one of them asked, "May we help you, ladies?"

"You bet!" Irene replied, handing over the map to the two young men and at the same time explaining to them what it was we were looking for. The bespectacled one peered down the map, looked up at the street signs, looked down at the map again, pointed the church's location to his companion, conferred with him and then instructed us to cross the street and walk towards the right. They even mentioned some landmarks. For who can really remember any of the long and tongue-twisting street names like Kungstradgardsgatan, Stallgatan or Nybrokagen?

"Thank you so much for your help. By the way are you residents of the city?"

"No, we're tourists."

"Where are you from?"

"England. How about you, guys?"

"We're from the U.S.A."

"Okay, stay safe."

"You, too. Thank you."

After a few minutes walk, we sensed that we were nowhere near any of the landmarks which they described.

Irene studied the map again. "Folks, turn left." She ordered us. "They gave us the wrong directions." We turned left. We came upon a city park. A young man was busy setting up tables and chairs in front of a small restaurant. We showed him the name of the church. He pointed out to us a building right across the street. A foreigner would have been very fortunate if he found the church by himself. The row of buildings consisted of a sequence of multistory business apartments. The church is hidden behind the facade of a former dwelling house and the only visible sign is a cross at the main doorway.

It was exactly 9:30 a.m. when we entered St. Eugenia's Catholic Church, the oldest Catholic parish in Sweden, founded in 1837. We were nearly late for Mass.

Lesson learned: *"When the blind lead the blind, confusion may not be too far behind."*

# ROUGHED UP IN A TENDER

The tiny Tender in the rough seas

Visby is a fortified city on the Swedish island of Gotland, the land of the ancient Goths. Excavations have produced remains of stone age people, thus showing that this place was inhabited more that 8000 years ago.

It is a UNESCO World Heritage City which has retained its medieval character. Its multi-faceted culture resulted from the mixture of influences by the Swedes, Danes, Germans, and the Vikings.

The cruise excursion for that day described Visby as the "City of Roses and Ruins" and as "Sweden's sunniest vacation destination". This city has the most sun-hours in all of Sweden.

Roses and ruins? Yes, we agree with that. Streets lined with blooming roses were a beauty to behold. The ruins, some of which are still being used, evoked a feeling of being transported in time.

Sunniest? Our experience negates this description.

Our day started with some light showers. As expected our huge cruise ship couldn't dock at Visby itself. It was anchored about a mile away from land. Thus were we (I, for sure, was,... and I assume so were the rest of us.) introduced to new expressions: Tender, Tender Ticket, Tendering.

Since I never had anything to do with nautical terms, the word "tender", to me, had a principal meaning that didn't go beyond the kitchen stove as in, "The beef is tender" or "Boil the carrots until they are tender."

Once in a while it presented to me a secondary meaning that is more emotional than what is happening in the kitchen area, as when Elvis Presley sings with full emotion, "Love me tender, love me sweet..."

Tender, in this present setting, I later surmised, referred to the life boat that would bring us ashore. Tender ticket is the slip of paper that gives us passage from the ship to the tender. Tendering is the process of transporting us from the ship to the shore and vice -versa.

Thus, armed with this new knowledge, we departed from our mother ship with great expectations for the day's visit to the continuously inhabited medieval town. We walked through cobblestone streets; enjoyed the beautiful rose gardens; visited medieval churches, Vikings' harbor, and ruins of a once fortified city.

Rain was continuously pouring during all this time. But with our rain gear consisting of umbrellas, raincoats, and hooded jackets, we continued our tour and enjoyed every moment of it.

Then it was time to go back to the cruise ship. When we reached the berthing area, a huge crowd had gathered. All were waiting for the tenders to transport us.

After about a half hour wait, it was our turn to board one of the tenders. Having found no more empty seats when I boarded, I took a seat on the steps that led to the roof. "No problem", I said to myself. "It's only a ten to fifteen minute trip."

How wrong I was! First, we noticed that our boat wasn't moving forward. Then we saw that our Filipino captain was having trouble with the malfunctioning windshield wiper. Being the innovative Filipino that he is, he made a windshield wiper out of a small towel. This he used to wipe the glass which continuously became cloudy. At certain times, he opened the hatch over his seat to take a peek at the sea. Naturally, he got drenched with the pouring rain. This continued for about an hour. Eventually, he turned around and announced to all of us who had been patiently waiting and wondering why we were not moving forward, that he was awaiting orders from the ship as to when we could leave port. Due to the strong winds and rough seas, it was difficult and unsafe for the small tender to align with the big ship. Hence, transferring the passengers from the little boat to the ship, while the boat was being tossed mercilessly by the huge waves, was gravely dangerous.

During this long wait the unthinkable happened to me. I needed to go... just got to go ... got to go! I felt the call of nature at the time we boarded. More than one hour has gone by and I was in considerable distress.

Finally, the captain's assistant walked in from the bow where he had been enduring the incessant rainfall all this time. Hoping that they might have some 'secret' room somewhere for the crew, I asked him. My hopes were crushed when he said there was nothing inside. "But there's one on the roof," he said. For a while I thought it was true. I was willing to go up. It turned out he was trying to be funny. But in my state of suffering I sensed no humor whatsoever.

Fortunately, within a few minutes our captain announced that he received the go signal. That was the best news I heard that day.

We left port quickly and started sailing smoothly despite the continuous rain and wind. But as soon as we got into the wide open sea, our boat literally rolled with the waves; sometimes rolling on its side pushing us to the left then back to the right; sometimes lurching forward then suddenly leaning backward. The hatch above the stairs where I was sitting cracked open. I got soaked to the skin. The plastic "curtains" which covered the side doors flapped wildly with the wind. Some passengers were shrieking and screaming with fright as the little boat bravely sailed forward. The captain was undaunted by the broken windshield wiper. To him that little towel was sufficient to make him see through the fog.

I saw some passengers grabbing life jackets. As for me, my mind was preoccupied with my physical needs. I wasn't afraid of what would happen to the tumbling life boat at all. That came later. At that moment my only concern and prayer was to get myself to the nearest toilet.

At last... at long last... our tiny boat was beside the ship! Cruise personnel were waiting to give each of us a hand as we managed to jump aboard to safety. As I swiped my SeaPass card I begged the young man to give me directions to the nearest toilet.

I probably looked so miserable that instead of giving me directions he personally led me to the nearest facility. Then and there my heart overflowed with a two-fold thanks to God: thanks for having landed us safely and thanks for the ladies room!

At the ship's Centrum I joined a couple who were watching the approaching tenders. I was aghast at the sight of the tender which looked like a miniature plastic toy rolling in all directions subject to the relentless lashing of both winds and waves.

"Oh, God, I was out there a while ago!" Only then did I grasp the danger that we had just been through. It didn't help that the elderly gentleman explained to me that tenders are designed to readily lean or roll in response to the wind, hence safe even in extreme weather conditions. From where we were seated we watched the life boats being tossed at sea. We saw how the boats mightily fought their way back to the ship. It was not a pleasant sight.

I limply slumped on a nearby seat and weakness settled down through my whole body. I was belatedly scared to death!

Visby, oh, Visby!!! You were once a stranger to me but now you're indelibly etched in my memory. For how can I possibly forget you? You, who tenderly tortured me!

Lesson learned: *"Travel opens the mind not only to new worlds, but also to new words and experiences."*

# IN SEARCH OF THE HOLY CHAIR

Our Lady of the Miraculous Medal

The Knights searched for the Holy Grail. I, on the other hand, searched for the Holy Chair.

It all began with a serendipitous find of a 58-year-old pamphlet which came tumbling down my not-so-oft used bookcase. I was searching for a book of saints which my son Jose gave me as a birthday gift a couple or so years ago. I wanted to read about St. Jeanne d'Arc before leaving for our pilgrimage / tour of Southern France in April 2011.

Our itinerary was to fly to Nice, and from there proceed to the rest of the French Riviera including Eze, Antibes, Juan-les-Pins, Cannes, on to the Principality of Monaco, then to the city of Paris and its outskirts in Versailles. This was the "tour" part of the trip. The "pilgrimage" part included the Shrine of the Immaculada Concepciou in Lourdes, the Shrine of St. Therese the Little Flower in Lisieux; the Shrine of St. Jeanne d'Arc in Rouen; the Cathedrals of Notre Dame and Sacre Coeur in Paris; and the Chapel of Our Lady of the Miraculous Medal, also in Paris. As I pulled the book off the shelves, a blue covered pamphlet, yellowed with age, fell on the floor in front of me.

I wondered as to whose it was; or whether it was given to me sometime in the past; or if any of my friends left it during a visit to my home; or if it came from one of the priests at the rectory where I used to work. ... I simply could not remember.

My eyes popped out as the cover announced: Our Lady of the Miraculous Medal, Rue du Bac, Paris, France. I knew about the Miraculous Medal. But I did not know much about St. Catherine nor about the details of the apparitions nor about how the medal was designed.

With much care, I picked up the old pamphlet and gently leafed through the brittle and aged pages. It was dated 1953. That was more than half a century ago. I voraciously read about St. Catherine Laboure and the apparitions of the Blessed Mother to this holy nun.

In Paris, finding the Sacre Coeur and Notre Dame Cathedrals was no problem at all. Everyone ... anyone ... who visits Paris knows where to find them. These structures are not only imposing but famous as well. So, who would not be able to locate them? On the other hand, the chapel on 140 Rue du Bac which was previously the medieval Hotel de Chatillon before its consecration in 1815, had no majestic dome nor lofty spires. But with Emilie, the vibrant, sociable, amiable, easy-to-get-along-with physician in the group leading the way, we found it in no time.

As we approached the shrine, I could feel my pulse quickening and my heart thumping with excitement as I anticipated the culmination of my search for the Holy Chair.

Finally, there it was in front of the altar on the right side apse of the church! It was a simple wooden chair, upholstered in blue. There was nothing visibly extraordinary about it. But what made it so very extra special was that our Blessed Mother, as she appeared to St. Catherine in her human form, sat on this chair for more than an hour while she discussed with the holy nun numerous topics ranging from prayer, conversion, penance, forgiveness and love; to the design, production, distribution and significance of the miraculous medals.

I imagined the Blessed Mother comfortably seated, like any mother would be when she converses lovingly and intimately with her child. Then I imagined St. Catherine kneeling ... or perhaps sitting ... at her feet, listening intently as any child with a heart open for instructions and receptive of guidance from her mother would.

I am aware of other officially recognized miraculous apparitions of our Blessed Mother: at Guadalupe in Mexico; at Lourdes in France; and at Fatima in Portugal. In all of these miracles, I had the impression that Our Lady was always standing. This is the only apparition that I know of where she sat down for a long time. It struck me as a symbol of her oneness with us humans ... especially as we grow older ... when we would rather sit down than stand up during a lengthy animated conversation.

I searched for the Holy Chair ... and, with God's help, I found it!

The Blessed Virgin Mary sat on this
chair during her third apparition to
St. Catherine Laboure

Lesson learned: *"Search and you will find!"*

# A TEACHABLE MOMENT

No doubt about it, Eiffel Tower is a beauty during the day. It is dazzling at night. The glittering lights emanating from this lofty structure draw people towards her. So were we, like moths drawn towards light, drawn towards her.

Ellen and her son Jeb, Emilie, Long, my daughter Bamba and I braved the cold windy April night to join the long line of tourists who wanted to experience the exhilaration at the top of this formidable man-made structure which soars above the city of Paris.

The line to the ticket booths was not only long. It was slow-moving as well. But being outdoors in open space, you did not feel confined. And it was orderly. So was the line to the first stage elevator which takes you to the mid-section of the tower.

In contrast, due to the limited floor area, the line at the mid-section which leads to the second stage elevator which takes you to the top, was congested. Despite this, order was kept by the steel guide bars which zigzag through the limited space as it directs the multitude in a single file towards the second elevator's door. The movement was at snail's pace. But this posed no problem. From this vantage point, the sight of the sparkling lights of grand and exciting Paree below kept us far from being bored.

The sounds among the throng reminded me of the Tower of Babel. Various groups of people spoke in different tongues. Some accents were familiar, some words were intelligible, but most were

Greek to me as Greek could be. An elderly plump lady with two teenage daughters continuously chatted in Spanish; we spoke in Tagalog; I heard someone speak Arabic; another in Russian; somewhere someone was speaking Chinese; and a bunch of teenagers were having fun kidding each other in their unmistakably American accent. It seemed like the whole world of languages was up there at the top of Tour Eiffel! The cacophony of numerous spoken dialects was both amusing and entertaining.

Photo "addicts" that we are, even in the tight spaces between the steel guide bars, we were snapping pictures of each other. A sweet smiling, svelte Mexican girl offered to take our group picture. We delightedly and thankfully accepted her offer and posed for posterity.

The line continued to move on in slow motion. Then out of nowhere, right in front of us, where the steel bar made a U-turn, a young lad with his leg straddled atop the bar said, "May I jump over to join my friends out there?" He was pointing at two teenage girls who were way ahead of us.

Not one of us replied. But Ellen looked at him with a dagger-like look, wordlessly saying, "Mind your manners, young man. Stay in line as everyone else does!"

The kid spoke again. "Can I jump over?" The two girls started giggling. Still we kept silent. We simply stared at him. Another group of girls, standing far behind us, yelled at him, saying, "Go ahead. They don't speak English. But can't you see how they look at you, like they're going to kill you? Just jump!"

He jumped! We simply shook our heads in dismay at his uncouth behavior.

But that was not the end.

By some strange coincidence, on our way down, our group literally bumped into him and his two girl friends at the most inconvenient place. We were squeezed together within the confining walls of the elevator. The kid and his two female friends were standing face to face with Emilie.

"Hi, where are you, guys, from?" was Emilie's unexpected query. I heard them gasp. They realized that we did speak English.

"From upstate New York," was their chorused reply.

"And, how about you?" They directed their question to Emilie.

"I'm from New York, too. ... Long Island, New York. And we speak English up there, too!"

As if on cue, I jumped into the conversation convinced that being an elderly woman I had the right to teach these young kids some good manners. "You were the kid who jumped the line up in the tower, right? Contrary to what your friends told you, we do speak fluent English." I could see his face turning red as a beet. He couldn't say a word.

The two girls tried to come to his rescue. "We didn't say that," they protested.

"Sure, you didn't say that. Your companions way back in the line where he came from ... they were the ones who prodded him to jump."

Then addressing the young man again, I said, "If I may say so, young man, mind your manners wherever you may be. That will make you feel good and look good all the days of your life."

The elevator door opened. We all left ... each to our own parts of the world.


Lesson learned; *"When a teachable moment jumps right before you, grab it!"*

"*Travel is more than the seeing of sights; it is a change that goes on, deep and permanent, in the ideas of living.*"

Miriam Beard

## LOURDES, THE SECOND TIME AROUND

Between the years 1995 and 2011, some things have changed. Surprisingly, much has remained the same.

The gift shop is still there. So is McDonald's. Probably the restaurant is there, too. But for the life of me I can't remember what or where it was. Nor do I remember the face of the kind shopkeeper who kept her store open beyond her usual schedule and who escorted us away from a fast dinner at McDo. *(Author's note: see Dinner at Lourdes, page 151).*

Lourdes, the place and its structures, hasn't changed much in sixteen years. Evidently the change was not of Lourdes. It was more between Lourdes and me.

My first tour in 1995 was a very quick one. We shunned the crowd; we prayed by ourselves; and that was it. My eyes saw Lourdes, but my heart and soul did not.

This time we did not shun the crowds; we prayed together the Holy Rosary, attended the Masses, joined in the processions, knelt at benediction, walked and meditated the Via Dolorosa, dipped at the baths. We joined the multitude of pilgrims who came from far and wide and who patiently lined up to silently, reverently and prayerfully walk towards the niche on the massive rock where the Mother of God appeared to what the people of her time called "the crazed little girl of Massabielle". We lingered in the proximity of the tiny well which the young girl Bernadette dug with her bare hands and from which a stream of healing waters now emanates. We drank and collected some stream water from the faucets.

The congregation convened for the evening's prayer of the Holy Rosary at a candlelight procession. Hundreds of sick, weak, frail, disabled and infirm were seated on their blue wheel chairs, fingering their rosary beads and joining the prayers, each in his own dialect. They were made comfortable and protected from the early evening chill by multi-colored lap blankets. Either a family member or a volunteer aide gently pushed them among those who could walk.

Undoubtedly the very sick are still being tested in the crucible of human suffering. Yet in most of them you can see a kind of peace and serenity brought about by their unshakable faith and hope. This is the "kind of peace which the world cannot give!"

As for the hundreds upon hundreds of volunteers who are identified by their dainty and color-coded scarves, or by the ID cards hung around their necks, or by the badges around their arms, they, too, have come from all corners of the globe to serve in numerous ways. In fact I met a fellow Filipino-American who was

Praying the rosary at the candlelight procession

volunteer for the first time and whose role was to help pilgrims locate the different areas which they wanted to visit.

What can be more moving than seeing young girls, perhaps in their early teens, carrying pitchers of water from the stream, walking among the wheelchair bound and offering each a re-fill of refreshing cold water? Their compassion was evident as shown by the care with which they refilled the cups carried by each sick person with cords around their necks, and then helping them to take a sip from their cups.

I approached an English-speaking Frenchman and inquired, "What do those armbands signify?" I was pointing to numerous able-bodied men and women wearing armbands designating them as "Montfortaine". I learned from him that they are health professionals including doctors, nurses, hospital staff and other volunteers from various parts of France who organize to serve the sick and the pilgrims. They are named in honor of Saint Louis Marie de Montfort who is best known for his devotion to the Blessed Virgin.

It is amazing how Bernadette Soubirous, a simple, naive, poor and powerless peasant girl was chosen by our Blessed Mother to move the world to its knees in prayer! It is amazing how to this once secluded corner of the globe in the Pyrenees, in the grotto of Massabielle, beside the rushing waters of the river Gave de Pau, millions are drawn by faith and hope for healing, or return to serve as volunteers in love and thanksgiving. Amazing! Simply amazing!

Although I did not personally witness any visible miraculous healing during my pilgrimage, deep in my soul I am certain that somewhere in that crowd someone has undergone some kind of profound and inexplicable physical and/or spiritual transformation.

The spiritual aspect of Lourdes impacted powerfully on me during this visit. To me Lourdes was different ... the second time around. I could not help but wish that, if only the kind of faith, service, cooperation, selflessness, compassion, decency, prayerfulness, and understanding that brings about order, peace, and healing in this sanctified place could be translated throughout the world, then war will have no place to thrive. If only ... !

The sick in procession on their
wheelchairs

Lesson learned: *"The miracle of a Mother's love and God's unending grace is evident in this holy place.*

196

# THE POWER OF A VOWEL

Fredericksborg Castle

Copenhagen, the capital city of Denmark, is also its economic and financial center.  It is a city where ultra modern architecture like the Black Diamond building stands side by side with medieval palaces like the Christiansborg Palace, and churches like the large domed Marble Church.  The city is also home to numerous parks and gardens of which the most visited is that of the Rosenborg Castle.  Museums such as that of Hans Christian Andersen and amusement parks like the Tivoli are also well known tourist attractions.

The famous Canal Tour appeals to a multitude of visitors.  During our boat ride Bamba and Bel had a very friendly conversation with another tourist who enthusiastically encouraged them to visit another palace.  They understood it to be Frederiksberg  Palace.

After the canal tour we took a bus and asked the driver if it will take us to Frederiksberg.  He said "Yes. I'll tell you when to get off."  Soon we reached the destination.  There was no palace in sight.  We were at Frederiksberg Alle, that is  Frederiksberg Street.

Bel approached a middle aged man who looked like a resident.  He told us to walk towards the City Hall, then to take a bus from there.  He also said that the palace is beside the zoo.  We followed his directions.  Unexpectedly, we found Stroget, the famous pedestrianized business section.  At least, we enjoyed the walk through Stroget to the City Hall.

At the end of Stroget we boarded bus 6A.  We got off when

we saw that we were approaching the zoo. We passed by what looked like a palace gate. While some of us stopped in the shade, not wanting to enter the zoo, I went back to the gate. It was open. I went in and asked the uniformed guard. "Sir, is this Frederiksberg Palace?"

"Yes, Ma'am, it is."

"How do we get inside then?" I asked.

"I'm sorry but the palace is closed to visitors. It is now military property. But you can visit the gardens."

"Thank you. Thank you, sir."

With this information, I went back to the group. In my absence, Bel, Bamba and Long were able to get some other information. It turned out that in Denmark there are two royal residences with almost identical names. One is Frederiksberg Palace (1699) which served as the royal family's summer residence until the mid-1800s, but which later on (1869 to present) housed the Royal Danish Army Officers Academy. It is adjacent to the Copenhagen Zoo. The other is the Frederiksborg Castle which is located in Hillerod, a place about an hour train ride from Copenhagen. The castle is built on three small islands in the middle of Palace Lake. It has a large formal garden reminiscent of the gardens of Versailles. It is now the Museum of National History.

Frederiksborg is what we wanted to see; Frederiksberg is where we were directed to go.

Wow! See what one vowel can do?

Lesson learned: *"Don't just cross your T-s and dot your I-s. Take care of your O-s and E-s as well."*

# TRUE CIVILITY

The Canals of Copenhagen

Weather-wise, it was a truly lovely day! Thank God for this gift and blessing. We had planned a long day ahead. There was still a lot to be explored in the beautiful city of Copenhagen, Denmark.

Irene, the self-appointed guide for the day, ran to the nearby Tourist Information Center where she asked for directions. She was given a map. A young Dane in a green uniform who I believe was an employee of the city's tourism industry tried to help Irene figure out how to navigate the city's streets for a one day tour.

Meanwhile, Estela, the leader of our pack, decided to go to a hotdog stand to buy food for her husband Willy. There were so many choices. She pointed out her choice. The vendor rudely yelled at her, "Don't touch the food!"

Estela responded, "I am not touching the food. I am only pointing out my choice."

At this point Willy heard the raised voices so he went to see what's going on. "Don't you dare yell at my wife!" This was Willy's instant remark.

More words were exchanged between Willy and the irate vendor.

Without buying anything, and to avoid more argument, the couple, Willy and Estela, left the stand to join the rest of us.

The vendor, still fuming with anger, came out of his stand and continued to confront Willy. It looked like a bigger fight was just about to erupt! Cooler heads intervened. This included the young man in green. He spoke to the vendor in their dialect. The only word I understood was "America". Probably the young gentleman was explaining to him that we were tourists from the United States. (It's sad to say, but Filipinos in most European countries including Denmark are looked down upon because they are usually employed as domestic help. My guess is that this vendor is some kind of a bigot who looks down on our countrymen. Mind you, that's just my guess. I hope I'm wrong.)

After tempers settled down, the young Dane apologized to all of us for the vendor's uncouth behavior.

Before we could move away from that unfortunate area a most touching incident took place. A pretty young Danish woman with three children in tow approached our group and sincerely apologized. "I am very sorry for what happened. You (looking at Estela) did not do anything wrong. I was there and I saw everything that transpired. I do not want you to go back to your country with a bad impression of my country. That man's behavior is not what Denmark is."

That was a terrific display of civility! We were deeply touched.

Lesson learned: *"There is beauty in civilized behavior."*

# TRAVELING WITH AN ANGEL

As I journeyed on the highway of daily life, I found out that the roadway was seldom paved and smooth. There were potholes, big and small; road bumps, high and low; steep grades to climb; sudden downhill drops; hairpin curves; dangerous precipices on the side; rugged terrain; slippery ice; flooded streets.

During those perilous or uncomfortable seasons of the journey, I prayed for a guardian angel to guide me, to pull me out of the potholes and to keep me from falling off the precipice.

God sent me one. Like all angels, mine is invisible to everyone but me. He has no name. Unlike other angels, mine has no wings. Neither does he have a halo. But again, like all angels, he is always there when a need arises. And mind you, he is not there only for me but also for the numerous other humans who cross his path and need his help.

I have christened my angel, Nick, as in St. Nick or Santa Claus.

My angel has strong helping hands ... not literally, though. He is elderly like Santa Claus is elderly, but is strong enough to lug those heavy gift-laden bags at Christmas time. For Nick, Christmas time is all the time. His heart is as big as the world. Although he looks tough, speaks forcefully, acts sternly, remains distant at times, and is oftentimes domineering and difficult, that is just his facade. Beneath this forbidding mask is a truly gentle, soft, kindhearted and generous person. Honesty and integrity are the bedrock of his life. He has been aptly described as a "diamond in the rough."

Nick appeared to me many years ago in a church which I attended upon arriving in this venerable country, the U.S.A.

He began to evidently be my angel when my youngest son immigrated to this country. There was a problem in his entry documents. I asked for help and he came to our rescue.

Years later another son became a victim of workplace discrimination. It was a sickening experience for him and for me. Without hesitation, Nick was there to help. For months on end he labored without recompense until the case was won.

I was in an accident. I must have taken a wink while driving. He was there in a moment's notice.

My grandson had a significant medical problem. We tried by ourselves but we couldn't find a specialist for his needs. With a few calls, Nick found a great doctor. Soon enough my grandson was treated and turned out as healthy as one could possibly be.

My sister caught a severe strain of pneumonia. I tried to get an immediate doctor's appointment for her. After three rejections, I called Nick for help. Fifteen minutes was all he needed to get an appointment. Within an hour a physician saw her, diagnosed and treated her. His immediate response and excellent treatment negated the need for hospitalization. My sister quickly and fully recovered.

Racquel's case as an injured passenger in a car accident was stagnant for almost two years. With a few calls, Nick moved it. Racquel's case went swiftly through the bureaucratic rigmarole, and ended with a hefty award of a good sum of money.

My daughter-in-law's father had a work-related problem which I personally did not understand. Angel Nick was there to resolve it in a jiffy.

Our parish church had many problems. Not in the spiritual realm, but in the fiscal and legal. Certainly, Nick, the problem solver, was always there ... any time of the night or day. It was like he was on duty for his beloved church 24 hours a day, 7 days a week. Needless to say, the problems were always solved. He never asked for a dime for his services.

Numerous parishioners ... too many to mention ... have asked for his assistance and were helped with definitively positive results.

My daughter had a really big problem. She felt helpless. I, too, was helpless. We had absolutely no knowledge about this process of going through the maze of red tape involved. Who did we turn to? Who else but Nick. For more than a year he labored to put the problem to rest. He succeeded. A big thank you and a grateful heart were all we could give him back.

There was a young man. He needed help ... much help ... . He was helped. He changed from an irresponsible C student to a responsible student who landed on the honor roll of his college. Who pushed him on? Who inspired him? Who mentored him? My angel; our angel.

Angel Nick is there, not only for big reasons but for small but significant reasons as well.

Remember the snowstorm of December 2010? Knowing that my daughter and I cannot handle by ourselves the snow shoveling after that brutal snowfall, Angel Nick came to help. No, not him personally. Like I told you, he is as old as Old St. Nick. Shoveling is beyond the capability of his years. Determined to help, he walked around the neighborhood in deep snow. He found four fine teenage helpers. They came and cleaned the snow off our driveway, sidewalk and cars.

Even for the mundane and minute tasks of everyday life, he was ever-present to offer his helping hands. The roof leaked, the faucet leaked, the sink clogged, doors won't lock, the trees needed trimming, the lawn required mowing, the awning was falling, the cars needed tuning. Who is there to offer a hand? No, not fair weather friends. Not even family. They're too busy with their own lives. Yes, a friend in need is a friend indeed. My angel friend was there for our needs. And if he can't do it himself, he will always find others to do what had to be done.

You might not believe this, but it's true. Not everyone around me likes old Angel Nick. They focus on the facade. Strange, but they refuse to see the heart within. Stranger still, some of those he helped banished him from their lives. Someday, as the journey continues, I hope that everyone Nick meets along the way will see him as I do.

Lesson learned: *"Angels may not have wings nor halos but they have the hearts and hands that help and protect."*

# THE SUBWAY SURPRISE

The Author with Irene and Bel at
St. Petersburg Metro

"Be sure to pack your lunch. This is a 13-hour nonstop 2009 excursion. Wear comfortable clothes and shoes. Bottled water will be provided on the bus. Tatiana, our guide, is our visa to St. Petersburg, Russia." Estela's reminders needed to be heeded. We were all set for a long day ahead.

*"Dobre utra! Da, da,* we are in St. Petersburg."

Tatiana started our day pleasantly by handing out complimentary books about St. Petersburg. What was most important in each book was her personal information. In the event that someone gets lost, (Hope to God nobody will!) there is a number to call.

This is the St. Petersburg that we visited: a city filled with gilded domes and towering spires, of palaces and museums, memorabilia of the Romanov monarchy, a mighty city set in splendor and opulence. Here life begins at 10:00 a.m. and continues deep into the night which in summer practically never grows dark.

Tatiana brought us in for a surprise. She led us to the Metro Station which was opened on November 15, 1955. But before we got there we saw the Moscow Triumphal Arch which depicted Russia's triumph over Napoleon. Stopping briefly, she warned us to move quickly, follow her closely and listen to her instructions. We were to ride the subway train! No wonder she gave us her phone number.

The train level is reached by way of an escalator that descended on one steep straight line 105 meters below street level. This reminded me of the escalator on Lexington Avenue in New York city, but this one descended far deeper into the belly of the earth. As soon as we stepped off the escalator we were astounded by the elegance of the subway system. This is something we did not expect. The subway was adorned with chandeliers, glass covered columns and sculptured walls. We looked closely at the sculptures. They depicted strong, healthy, beautiful young people. There was not a single elderly person there. That was how Communism was presented to the people: a perfect society for a perfect race. Wish it were true!

Cameras started clicking. The flashes were magnified in the semi - darkness. A burly man reached out to Tatiana and spoke to her in a somewhat rude manner. *"Da, da,"* was all we heard from Tatiana. The man left and Tatiana explained to us that flash photography was prohibited.

"Get on the next train. Get out at the second stop!" We did as ordered. We had more surprises at the next stop. The subway in St. Petersburg is probably like no other subway in the entire world. We saw more exquisite decorations and typical Soviet artwork and designs. But of course the "hammer and sickle" was clearly featured everywhere. It was built that way at the height of the Communist regime, to show off the "success" of Communism.

Life in the Metro was fast paced ... just like New York. But very much unlike New York, everything was spic and span! No clutter, no debris, no garbage ... only a museum-like atmosphere. It was a hidden beauty in the dark belly of the Communist world. This was a remarkable surprise!

Lesson learned: *"Beauty rises up like an obelisk even in the darkest of places."*

# TO HUMOR A CZAR

Peterhof Palace and
The Grand Cascade

Peterhof, Peter the Great's summer palace, was constructed in 1714 based on a sketch made by the king himself. Much has been added to the original structure especially during Catherine the Great's time. It is now a complex of numerous buildings, gardens, fountains and walkways. The main highlight is the Grand Cascade and the Samson Fountain which dramatically spouts gallons upon gallons of water through hundreds of jets that collect in a circular pool leading to the Sea Channel.

In July 2010 we visited the complex from the backdoor, that is, from the lovely formal gardens at which place you get the full view of the palace at the center, the St. Peter and Paul church to the right, and a tower topped by a double-headed eagle (Russia's symbol) to the left. Most of Peterhof has been restored close to, but not really the same as, its original grandeur. Despite that, you get numerous "wow!!! moments" ... you know, those times when you see something and no words come out of your mouth but the three - letter word "WOW", followed by a multitude of exclamation points.

We made our way to the ticket booth that allowed us entrance to the front porticos, the gardens and the rest of the more than a hundred other fountains. We joined the thousands of tourists who tried to find the best place to watch the fountain display. It was beautiful.

We walked around the rest of the grounds and saw numerous fountains of various shapes and sizes. One was a copy of the fountain at St. Peter's in Rome; another, constructed in the middle of what used to be the royal swimming pool, looked like the sun; another looked like a pine tree; one looked like a chess board; another consisted of several tulips spouting out jets of water. On this last one Jerry became a victim of Peter the Great's joke. A bench was situated under the shade. It looked so inviting to a tired tourist. Jerry accepted the invitation, took a seat; then suddenly jumped up! He got the seat of his pants wet!

"Gotcha, Jerry!" Peter must be laughing real hard watching Jerry jump up.

It was only after this incident that we learned that at least a couple of the fountains were actually designed for soaking unsuspecting visitors.

Lesson learned: *"A pair of wet pants to humor a king? That's not too much for him to ask of you!"*

# BOTTLED WATER IS SLIPPERY IN EGYPT

May 29, 2008, 9:00 a.m. We were all set for our horse carriage ride to Edfu Temple. This is the temple where the story of Horus' victory over Seth is depicted in the temple's walls. Fascinating!

Our daily routine starts with being sure that each of us carried at least one bottle of water. Today we each needed more than one because we expected an extremely hot day.

Just outside the hotel are street vendors selling bottled water. One of them approached me. He agreed to sell me 2 bottles for a dollar. I took one bottle and handed it to my daughter Bamba while I dug into my purse for a dollar bill. I found a 5-Egyptian pound which is valued more than a dollar. When I handed the bill to him, he changed the price to one bottle-for-five Egyptian pounds. Before I could complain he was gone!

Lesson learned: *"Sometimes the hand is quicker than the eye. So, watch out!"*

# TRAVELING ON A CAMEL'S BACK

Luxor Temple

Luxor Temple is an ancient complex located in the city of Thebes, close to the banks of the Nile River. It was built by King Amenhotep III during his reign (1390 - 1353 BC), was completed by Tutankhamun and Horemheb, and expanded by Ramses II.

Our mid-day morning visit to this colossal structure brought us way, ... way back in time. Among the numerous antiquities which are still standing in what is left of the kingdoms of bygone ages was a relief showing Rameses II proudly sitting on his throne. On another part, there was Alexander the Great presenting himself like a pharaoh.

A mosque sits on top of a temple. Its base is about three stories above the present ground level. On another part, some of the bas-reliefs are covered by frescoes. These changes show how the Pagan temple was used at some point in time as a Christian place of worship, then eventually as a Muslim mosque.

After visiting Luxor we set out for another "first" experience. We boarded the ferry to cross the Nile where the camels and the camel handlers and guides were waiting for us.

I asked Issa, my guide, a boy of about twelve who speaks fairly good English, "How do I get on the camel? It's too high for me."

"Don't worry, Ma'am. My camel, Aladdin, will kneel down and take you up." That was my first lesson in riding a camel.

So down Aladdin went on his knees, and up I climbed on his back. As Aladdin rose taking me higher and higher, I was clutching the reins tighter and tighter. Keeping my balance was a feat. Issa sensed my nervousness. "I'll be walking beside you and the camel, Ma'am. You will be safe." The assurance from Issa made me feel much more confident.

After each of us had been comfortably seated on the backs of the camels, our caravan, led by a horse-riding escort, paraded through the main streets of the village. Vehicular traffic was stopped for us. Our escort acted as the traffic police. He led us through the fields of sugar cane, corn fields, and banana groves, then unto the narrow alleys of another tiny village. Then suddenly there was a steep downward slope in the alley. I became very nervous. My body leaned forward in the same direction the camel was going. I thought I would fall. Just in time I heard Issa yelling, "Lean baaaaaacccckkk!" I did. I regained my balance and the smooth camel ride continued. From then on, at every downward incline, I simply leaned back!

Our Caravan

Lesson learned: *"Sometimes it is best to go against the tide. Going with the flow isn't always the smartest thing to do."*

# PAPYRUS BOOKMARKS

Our tour of Egypt in 2008 was blessed with a guide who was not only knowledgeable but also caring and concerned about our safety and well-being. Hanan warned us, among other things, against buying from vendors without her knowledge and consent. She knew that some of the vendors take advantage of tourists who have no idea about the true worth of the goods they buy.

Carmela, one member of our group, started having problems with her left foot on the second day of the tour. But she was such a bubbly and unstoppable woman. She never wanted to be left behind. She did not allow her foot problem to get in the way of her sightseeing experiences.

I think it was the fifth day of the trip. We were in Luxor where the temperature rose to 105 degrees. The heat aggravated the pain in Carmela's foot. So she decided to stay on the bus while the rest of us braved the sun's rage as we roamed the Temple of Luxor.

Despite the sweltering heat, we continued walking through the temple. We were informed that this must have been the place where Joseph and the Pharaoh saved the grains before the famine and where Joseph met and forgave his brothers who sold him as a slave when he was a child. Soon thereafter, we marched back to the refuge of our air conditioned bus.

Carmela excitedly called our attention, "Look, girls! Look at what I got. These are papyrus bookmarks, eight for only ten dollars."

Hanan's eyes widened. "Carmela, how much did you say you got them for?"

"Eight for ten dollars," Carmela proudly exclaimed, thinking that she got a real good bargain.

"Who sold it to you?"

Carmela pointed to the young man standing with his wares beside the bus. With lightning speed, our guide got off the bus, called the man and spoke to him in Arabic. Although we couldn't understand a word, we knew that Hanan was furious. We tried to guess what the furor was all about. We couldn't, not until she called out, "Carmela, here are two more bookmarks and your nine dollars back. This man unfairly overcharged you."

"You mean this should be ten for a dollar?"

"You bet! These are not real papyrus. Good enough for a souvenir, though. They look real."

Carmela was visibly happy. We were all amused at what happened.

The end result was that many of us bought the bookmarks for ten for a dollar. ... Not from the same vendor, though.


Lesson learned:  *"Listen to the advice of a wise woman."*

# A JOURNEY INTO THE BELLY OF THE EARTH

The six Pyramids of Giza

The Pyramids of Giza in Egypt have always fascinated me. And so it was with extreme excitement that I set foot on the desert sands surrounding the site. Based on the pictures I had seen, I thought that it would be enough to stand at a comfortable distance and view the magnificent and colossal structures. I was wrong.

Our Egyptian guide explained to us that the best way to have a full experience is to do two things. First, take a ten-minute camel ride which would take you on a tour of all six pyramids. ... Six, yes, six; not three as we often see in the photographs of this famous and ginormous work of human hands.

Second, walk down into the depths of the Pyramid to see the ancient and exquisite tomb in there. "Be sure to carry a bottle of water. Remember that you are to go down into the belly of the earth. It is hot and humid. You have to crouch all the way down and up again. The clearance between the ceiling and the steps is very low." These were the admonitions given to us by our guide.

After the camel ride around the Pyramids, my close friend Carrie, a slim, physically fit petite lady, encouraged me to join her to explore what lies beneath this structure. "There won't be any problem with us crouching. I guess the clearance is high enough for our less than five feet statures." We both agreed.

While the other members of our group were still trying to make up their minds whether to venture or not, Carrie and I walked straight to the door at the northern side of the Pyramid. We were pleased with ourselves.

Upon entering the door we knew how wrong we were about our height. The clearance on the passageway was probably only four feet. We needed to crouch as we descended the numerous steps. I was halfway down. I started feeling thirsty, boxed in and nearly suffocated. I took a sip of water. My thirst was partially quenched, but the feeling of suffocation persisted. I continued walking down until I reached the first level where there was more than enough space to finally stand erect.

"Carrie," I called out. "Are you okay? I don't feel like I can go on. I'm going back."

"Are you sure? What if you rest a little bit? Perhaps you will feel better. But whatever is comfortable for you, do as you please. I'm going to explore these corridors."

"Okay, take care. See you later." With that I started my climb back up, still crouching, still panting, and still feeling the need for wide open spaces.

My journey to the belly of the earth was thus aborted. But the memory of that experience ... of having tried ... although I had failed to reach the final destination ... was, to me, success enough.

Lesson learned: *"I can accept failure, everyone fails at something. But I can't accept not trying."* *...Michael Jordan*

# ENGINEERS ARE WEIRD

The month was July. The year was 2008. We were a group of forty people from different parts of the USA. Our "sub-group" of Filipino travelers consisted of nine people. We were cruising the Nile River during our tour of Egypt. As in most cruises, it is the usual practice for us to occupy the same seat at dinner every night. However, during this one night, for some reason which I cannot remember, Marilou and I arrived a little late at the dinner area. Our seats had been taken. So we looked around for two vacant seats at another table.

We joined the group of Sue, Julia, their respective husbands, and another gentleman whose name I recall was Dan. They were in the middle of an animated conversation when we joined in and Dan was sharing his experiences when he was with the Air Force where, according to him, he worked with a good number of engineers. He was amusingly describing the engineers as a bunch of weird and nerdy people. Julia's husband shared this opinion and he said that was the reason why he decided to pursue an MBA instead of an M.S. in Engineering. When Marilou and I heard this, we looked at each other quizzically.

Before more damaging descriptions of engineers could be exchanged, with a smile on my face I joined the conversation and asked Dan. "Did you say engineers are weird and nerdy?"

"Yeah, most of them are," he replied. "I worked with a lot of them for a considerable period of time and I found them to be so," he further explained.

"Well, I'm sorry to hear that, but unfortunately you are speaking to one," I commented.

Then Marilou added, "Evelyn, aside from being an engineer herself, and I ... I'm a chemist ... have intermingled and worked with engineers all our lives. We were engineering professors back in the Philippines. Hence, we have taught thousands of engineering students during our lengthy teaching careers at the university. We didn't find them to be weird and nerdy at all. In fact they were fun to be with because of their refreshing sense of humor."

With a crimson countenance, Dan uttered, "Oh, next time I better watch my mouth!" The conversation then abruptly shifted to a new topic.

Lesson learned: *"Whenever possible, reserve negative comments to yourself."*

ꗦ

## THE DRIVER

March 21, 2005, The Summer Palace.
Our map showed that the famed Summer Palace in Beijing, China wasn't too far away. We planned to take a taxi to our destination. Since not one of us knew how to speak Chinese, the hotel manager wrote down the name and address of our destination and instructed us to give it to the taxi driver. We did as we were instructed. We boarded a taxi and showed the driver the name of the place as written down for us by the hotel manager. We were merrily on our way.

A few minutes after we left the hotel we noticed that we were driving in circles and that the driver kept shaking his head. Eventually he turned off the taxi meter and kept on driving. After a while a smile came upon his face and he started nodding his head like he was saying "Yes! I got it!" He then turned on the taxi meter. We were so impressed by the honesty of this driver. Nowhere in the world have I met a taxi driver as honorable as him.

We walked the landscaped gardens of the Summer Palace, under shady trees beside the lake. We enjoyed the beautiful scenery, the temples, the walkways and the arched bridges. There was a long covered breezeway known as the "Long Corridor" whose ceiling was painted lavishly with colorful Chinese designs. We sat down on one of the benches. Fanned by the cool breeze, we breathed in the fresh air and imagined the extravagant lifestyles of the emperors and empresses of long ago. For a while we stepped back many generations in time.

But our admiration and fond memories of that honest driver never left our minds ... and never will.

Lesson learned: *"Honesty is the best policy ... no matter where ... no matter when."*

# THE GREAT DINNER AFTER THE GREAT WALL

The Author at the Badaling Great Wall

Starting in the 5th century B.C. the Chinese were already building walls to protect their borders. The walls were constructed primarily by ramming earth and gravel between wooden frames. In 221 B.C. the Qin Dynasty was established. The first emperor of China, Qin Shi Huang, ordered the construction of new walls to protect his empire from the intruding Xiongnu warriors. Stones were used to build the portions of the walls situated over mountain ranges; rammed earth was utilized to build those parts located on the plains. Unfortunately, most of these walls have eroded and very few sections remain today.

The Han, Sui, and Jin dynasties which followed continued the task of wall building to provide a defense against northern invaders. The construction of the Great Wall, as it stands today, was brought about during the Ming Dynasty (1502) to protect the empire from violent attacks by the nomadic Manchurian and Mongolian tribes. Bricks and stones were used instead of rammed earth.

The Great Wall is estimated to be 8,851 kilometers long. At the inner side of the wall there are arched doors that lead you to stone stairs that take you to the top of the wall. At intervals of 300 to 500 meters, there are fortresses. These were used for guarding and fighting.

A great deal of restoration work was done to the Badaling section in 1957. It is the section that is visited by millions of tourists which include humble people like us, as well as the great and mighty leaders of the world. This ancient military defense structure has an average height of 8 meters. It stands at an elevation of 1,000 meters. The top of the wall is wide enough to allow approximately ten persons to walk side by side.

The drive to the Badaling Great Wall, which is about 70 kilometers from the city, was about one and a half hours. Upon leaving our bus, the guide instructed us to purchase a ticket for the Biconvex Pulley ride to the wall. The vehicle consisted of a single row of multicolored high back seats on top of a monorail. We had to climb to the seats and strap ourselves to them. A pulley pulled it forward and before long we found ourselves in a tunnel that gradually ascended. At the end of the tunnel we got off and found ourselves right there on one of the archways that led to the stone steps which I mentioned earlier.

The sight was spectacular! As we walked on top of one of the living landmarks of ancient civilization we stopped a great number of times for picture taking ... of course! Although the sun was pouring its heat and light upon us, the cold wind kept us holding on to our jackets as if we were holding on for dear life.

From where we were, we could see the wall extending both ways ... far beyond where our eyes could see. It was an unforgettable majestic sight!

We returned to the city taking with us the indelible imprint of one of the world's greatest man-made superstructures.

Before going back to our hotel we decided to search for a place to eat. Everything was in Chinese. What else could we expect? We entered one of the restaurants. Fortunately, the menu had English translations. But they were unintelligible ... to us, that is. The two young waitresses tried their best to explain to us what food to order. But their means of communication was best described as sign language, not verbal communication.

As luck would have it, a young man at the next table noticed our predicament. He came to our rescue and explained what the waitresses wanted to say. He ended by ordering for us and explaining how the food was to be served and eaten. We learned that he was employed in a larger hotel which required his knowledge of English. We appreciated his help and thanked him.

After a not-too-long wait, our order was served ... rather, the young man's order was served to us. Now, we had another problem. What do we do with what and where do we mix what with what? Again the two waitresses noticed our naivete, nay, stupidity. They started to giggle but muffled their laughter. Without a word, they lifted up some of the food with tongs, dropped it into the boiling pot of water on the table; took it out again after a minute or so and placed it on our plates. Then they mixed some ingredients in little bowls and placed some of the resulting mixture over the food on our plates.

The young waitress helping me would have shoved the food into my mouth had I not nodded my head to indicate that I knew what to do next. I fed myself.

What an experience!

Lesson learned: *"Truly, there is much to be learned out there. Even feeding oneself may be a problem."*

# THE TEMPLE AND THE THEATER

Temple of Heaven, Beijing, China

My visits to two architectural expressions, one in China and the other in Jordan, were half a decade apart. I was extremely surprised how two structures from two completely different cultures and two different eras had one common invisible but very impressive feature.

March 22, 2005.

I visited the Temple of Heaven (Tiantan) in Beijing, China. The temple complex was constructed from 1406 to 1420 during the reign of the Yongle Emperor. This Temple is not only a holy place where the Emperor prayed for bountiful harvests. It is also one of the architectural wonders of Beijing. The huge circular building is said to be completely wooden and was built with not a single nail.

The magnificent triple-gabled circular building built on three levels of intricately carved marble stone base could be easily seen from our hotel. We decided to walk to the site. It should have been a good mile walk were it not for the dust carried by the strong winds directly into our faces. I could feel the crunchy particles in my mouth. As a result we took a taxi for the rest of the distance.

The temple was grandiose and highly symbolic with names like "The Imperial Vault of Heaven", "The Hall of Prayer for Good Harvest" and "The Circular Mound Altar". The entire complex was surrounded by a double wall with a circular shape on the northern end. This represents Heaven. The wall around the southern end is squarish, representing Earth.

There are two special places on the circular wall. If one person stands on one of these places and a second person stands on the other, a soft whisper by one will be heard loud and clear by the other despite the considerable distance between the two locations.

We experimented and succeeded.

"Can you hear me? Where are we going for lunch?" I whispered.

My friend answered, "I hear you loud and clear. Let's go to McDonald's."

Thursday, November 25, 2010.

After a few minutes ride from the city of Amman in Jordan we reached Jerash to view the ruins of the ancient Greco-Roman city of Gerasa. From the highway I thought there was nothing there but the Arch of Hadrian (129 AD). We quickly climbed the stairs up to the level of the arch's base. Then lo and behold! A Roman city was waiting to be explored. It is reputed to be one of the best preserved Roman cities in the Near East. We walked on the Cardo or the main avenue running N-S into the beautiful Oval Plaza which was surrounded by a colonnade of First Century columns and a broad sidewalk. This must have been the shopping area. The tracks of chariot wheels are still visible on the pavement which was made of huge blocks of stone.

The Roman Theater at Jerash

We entered the meat market, a spacious rectangular area where animals were butchered and sold.

An E-W road called Decumanus intersects the Cardo at the Tetrapylon.

We saw the Temple of Artemis and numerous other incredible structures.

Ruins of a fountain with a lion spouting water into a huge round dish were found alongside the Cardo. This is the Nymphaeum where women

Our pilgrim group at the Nymphaeum

221

came to fetch water needed at home. There was a magnificent structure in this area. It is a concave (semi-circular) two story building. The majestic structure rightly deserved to be the background for our group picture. James, our guide, was kind enough to be the photographer.

A massive hippodrome stands intact and is still in use. In fact a show was scheduled for that afternoon. Emilie and a few others wanted to attend. But most of us, thinking about the heat and the swirling dust that will surely come up during the chariot race, decided against it.

We visited a large Roman theater. I think this was the South Theater, built around 90 AD. The monumental structure is almost completely intact. It is impressive not only because of what we could see but also because of what we could hear. The acoustics were extraordinary. There was a spot around the middle, called the echo point. The voice of one standing on it reverberates throughout the entire theater. There was absolutely no need for a microphone for a performer standing there. My daughter Bamba, an excellent vocalist, spontaneously sang a few lines of "Memories". She was applauded by fellow tourists, strangers to us, who were seated at the farthest end of the open theater.

Although the walls are far apart, there is a point where a whisper on one side can be heard clear as a bell from a considerable distance on the other side. This, of course, clearly reminded me of the Temple of Heaven in Beijing.

Bamba singing at the Roman Theater

Lesson learned: *"Two different cultures, two different structures, one humankind, united in a transcendent way!"*

222

# THE MEEK LAMBS WERE IN FOR A SURPRISE!

The Siq

The rose-red city of Petra in Jordan, a World Heritage Site, is a marvelous interplay of what nature and man can do to enhance each other's works of art.

We were not prepared for what we saw. Right from the start, even before the entrance to the siq, everything was splendid. The ruins of the monument were amazing. Then as we entered the siq, the stones suddenly turned into colorful pink with streaks of other colors. The siq is the mile long narrow gorge that leads into the city of Petra. The towering multicolored sandstone walls that rise on both sides of the siq range from 300 to 600 feet in height. In sharp contrast to the height is the narrowness of the gorge. In some areas, it is only 2 to 3 meters wide. Along the way there were niches, shrines and carvings.

It is believed that tectonic forces caused the sandstone rock to split thereby creating the rift. Its surface has been smoothened by wind and water. In addition to the wondrous and magnificent natural beauty of the siq, there is the amazing indicator of the incredible intelligence of the Nabatean people. Close to the base of the cliff, they built a waterway system complete with a filtering process. This was used to carry water to the city from a distant spring.

We had been walking for almost an hour admiring the superb natural beauty along the way while at the same time being regaled by the endless stories and explanations of our guide.

"Stay very close to the mountain wall." Like meek lambs, we followed his intense instructions.

After a few minutes another set of orders was given. "Now, walk in pairs." He pointed his laser light on the left side. "Walk very slowly. Try to read the inscription on the wall. If you can't see it from where you are, you may now cross over."

We looked intently at the rose colored wall of the gorge. Not one of us could see any writing on the wall. "We can't see any inscription."

"Are you sure you can't see it? Look again. Now, do you see it?"

"No, we don't see any."

"Of course you cannot see any. There isn't any inscription! Now, everybody, turn quickly to the right and follow me."

We turned, and there it was! The focal point of Petra, the spectacular, the magnificent "Treasury"; a mausoleum exquisitely carved out of the towering rose-red mountainside; a man-made structure that has withstood the test of time, wind, storm, heat, and other forces of nature.

A unison of voices made a loud "WOW! Oh, my God! Oh, my God! What beauty! What an amazing wonder!" Thus were we dramatically introduced to Petra's show window. The stunningly beautiful Treasury is a living testimonial to the artistry, architectural and engineering genius of the Nabatean people.

We lingered, walked around, and climbed up some rocky hills which looked like enormous piles of boulders that crumbled down in ages past. Then somewhere atop the rocky hills we found a magical colorful spot where the boulders were a rainbow of fascinating colors.

The Treasury

Lesson learned: *"What we saw this day transcended the descriptive powers of what Sir Winston Churchill referred to as ... 'The 26 carving tools of the English alphabet.'"*

# SYCAMORE NUTS?

The Sycamore Tree in Jericho

Our group of 35 pilgrims from the U.S.A. was on its way to visit another most historic biblical site. Our bus turned left at the junction in Aimog. This was the highway exit that brought us to the Oasis City of Jericho, the oldest and lowest city (1100 feet below sea level) in the world. Canaanites lived here about 8000 years before the inception of Christianity; hence, 10,000 years before the present time. This city has been continuously inhabited. It was the first city captured by the Israelites under the leadership of Joshua after they spent 40 years in the desert. The walls came tumbling down by the trumpets of the Israelites. Ancient Jericho is up in the hills. A wadi has washed down over time the walls of that ancient city.

The lush greenery in and around the city gives Jericho an extraordinary air of elegance compared to the barren desert beyond. Because of the fertile soil and the many springs that feed this oasis, there is a profusion of agricultural products coming from orchards, commercial sized gardens, palm groves, and other farm sources.

Upon entering the city, our bus momentarily stopped beside a huge towering ancient tree. It was the sycamore tree. We were reminded of Zaccheus the tax collector who, being short in stature, climbed the sycamore tree in order to see Jesus as He passed by. Then Jesus called him to come down for He was going to dine with Zaccheus in his house.

Jericho is also the place where Jesus healed a blind beggar.

"Folks, that sycamore tree is about 500 years old. That was not really the tree which Zaccheus climbed. It was the same kind of tree, though." That was our guide, Isaac, inadvertently dampening our enthusiasm about the sycamore tree.

A few more turns on the narrow streets brought us right in front of Elisha's Spring Fountain in the middle of the city.

Across from Elisha's Spring Fountain, under the shade of a few palm trees, a vendor was busy selling fruits and preserves. Carol, a member of our group, bought some sycamore nuts which she offered us to taste. They were delicious. A number of us went to buy several bags of them; some to be eaten when we returned to the bus and some to be brought home as an exotic food from the Holy Land. A few moments later I heard a comment. "These are peanuts within a crunchy dough. Don't they taste exactly like the Nagaraya peanuts sold in the Asian stores back in the U.S.A.?" I looked closely at the handful which I was about to pop into my mouth. Yes, they did look and taste like peanuts.

Up to now I am still getting nuts over the questions: Were they really sycamore nuts as in nuts of the sycamore tree? Or did the vendor give peanuts the brand name "sycamore nuts"?

I inspected the bags. There were no labels on them. Had we been had? That question is also driving me nuts!

Lesson learned: *"Buyer, beware. Otherwise you might be deemed NUTS!"*

# THE WEDDING FEAST IN CANA

In November 2010, thirty-five Filipino-Americans and Filipino-Canadian pilgrims left JFK airport in New York for The Holy Land. One of the places which the couples in our group looked forward to visit was Cana, the town of Jesus' first miracle, where He turned water into wine at a wedding feast.

The present church, which is under the care of the Franciscans, is believed, but with some degree of uncertainty, to be the spot where the miracle happened. After staying a while for some prayers at the upper church, we all went down to the lower part where, after we viewed the ruins of the 1600 year old Byzantine church, all the married couples assembled before Rev. Alex Barbieto, our chaplain. He led them in renewing their marriage vows. The rest of us single people became excited cameramen and witnesses to the "mass wedding" ceremony. It was such an emotional moment and love was definitely in the air. We could see the bleary-eyed couples as they repeated their "I do's" , some of which were said long ago and far away. Long ago, as in 45 years ago; far way as in a distant land in one of the islands in the Philippine archipelago. The "newly re-wed" couples marched out of the chapel to the tune of the "Wedding March" sang by the choir of unmarried "angels" from the group.

Directly across the street from the church was a store specializing in Cana wine. Isaac, our guide, had made previous arrangements with the store manager for our group to drop by the store and perhaps do some business with gullible tourists like us. Thirty-five shot glasses of authentic free samples of locally made Cana wedding wine were waiting for us. Thirty-five shot glasses were raised up in the air as a toast to the newly re-weds.

With just that one sip we must have gotten intoxicated. After making some purchases we simply left the store and walked away without our guide. Soon we saw the poor guy running after us. We were reprimanded thus, "Where are you going? I told you to wait for me outside the store."

"Sorry, Isaac, your people are mostly walking on cloud nine. Remember, they just got remarried!"

The wedding feast was celebrated at the Tiberias Royal Plaza Hotel by the Sea of Galilee. What a romantic place for a honeymoon! Except that because it was Sabbath (sounds like "Shabat" when the locals say it) when we arrived, only one elevator was functioning normally and some of us had to climb 5 stories to our rooms.

At dinner, Kathy, one of the love-stricken newlyweds was at her best. She called a waiter and the following conversation ensued:

"Waiter, do you have tea?"

"No."

"No? Do you have coffee then?"

"No."

"Why?"

"It is Shabat."

"Okay, okay, give me shabat. I like shabat. I'll drink shabat." Whereupon the waiter stared at her in speechless bewilderment.

After a moment of awkward pause, Kathy, who was bewildered as to why the waiter was bewildered, spoke again. "Okay, give me hot water."

"Hot water? What will you do with it."

"I will drink it."

The waiter left. With a confused look on his face he came back with a teapot of hot water.

Thus Kathy's dinner ended with a cup of hot water. There was no tea nor coffee nor "shabat" for Kathy!

Lesson learned: *"The sound of laughter muffles cultural differences."*

# OLIVES

Olive Trees in the Garden of Gethsemane

I come from a tropical country, a land without olives. Although as a child I have eaten a few preserved olives from the bottle bought from the city which is four hours away by public transport from the rural town where I grew up, I had never seen a fresh olive.

The first time I saw olive plantations was on a distant hill during my trip to Italy. It was too far away for me to see the details of the tree, much less the fruit. Suffice that I saw what olive green really looks like. That was the first lesson I learned about olives; not a contrived copy of its color by Crayola, but by the visual experience of how it looked.

This may not be much of a lesson learned. Nevertheless, I appreciated the increment of knowledge that I have gained. Then piece by little piece I learned more about the olive.

Thirteen years later.

This time I came up close, very close to the olive trees in Gethsemane in the Holy Land. Not only did I see the tree. I saw the details of its leaves with silvery undersides, its branches, the trunk gnarled by hundreds of years of existence, the roots which were tenaciously holding on to the earth, and of course the fruits. Our guide gave us a sizable amount of information about the olives to show the importance of the tree and its produce.

The Bible mentions the olive branch carried by a dove to Noah to signify the end of the great flood.

The olive tree was sacred to the ancient Greeks. The olive wreath called the "Kotinos" was a symbol of greatness. It was an award given to ancient Olympic champions.

The olive branch remains a symbol of peace.

From the Christian perspective, the Garden of Olives was the place where Jesus prayed before He was betrayed by a kiss from Judas Iscariot.

The olive oil was and continues to be used for anointing the sick.

The gastronomic connoisseurs love the olive for its oils. The extra virgin oil comes from the first pressing of the fruits; the pure grade comes from the second pressing. These oils are scientifically accepted as the most healthful food oil.

The non-edible extracts were used to light the lamps and to grease the axles of the Roman chariots. Even the waste from all the pressing procedures is useful. When mixed with firewood it hastens ignition.

The olive wood comes to us in numerous art works, furniture pieces, exquisite carvings, holy rosaries, and other souvenirs.

Then of course the fruits come to our salads. The green fruits are often harvested in November. The unharvested fruits are left to ripen. By March they are ready to be harvested.

If the past is a foreshadowing of the future, who knows what the future holds for the great olive tree?

Before leaving the Holy Land, our guide gave each of us pilgrims a sprig of olive from his garden, a gesture of his thoughtfulness and a silent petition for a prayer for peace.

Lesson learned: *"Increments of knowledge span eons of ages gone, to eons of ages to come."*

# THE MIRACULOUS FALL OF RUDY

Our pilgrimage to the Holy Land brought us to the slopes of the Mount of Olives. Up and down we walked on the mountain to visit the numerous significant holy places in that area. Because the scenery was picturesque, everyone got busy taking pictures. Rudy and his wife Citas became overly engrossed in photographing each other and the magnificent historic city of Jerusalem.

Rudy was standing on top of a flight of ancient steps carefully focusing his camera to take a picture of Jerusalem's skyline when Citas called out to him. She wanted to take Rudy's picture with the holy city as the background. Rudy turned around to pose. Unaware that he was standing at the edge of the steps, he moved back a bit.

"Wham! Blam! Bog! Bog!" Rudy rolled down nine steps to the bottom of the hill.

The following is Rudy's own account of what happened next:

> " ... *Two steps backward and gravity took over. I rolled down about nine steps. When I got to the bottom, I still had my glasses on and Video cam in hand. It was a miracle. I got up, dusted my pants and climbed up the stairs. This happened in front of a lot of people. You should have seen the concern on their faces. I told them I'm OK and thanked them for asking. After a while I noticed a small cut on my hand and a slight pain on my side which disappeared after two days. That's it. Another unforgettable experience!"*

Lesson learned: *"Watch your back!"*

*"To travel is to live!"*

Hans Christian Andersen

# AT A LOSS FOR WORDS

Jerusalem:
The Old City and the Dome of the Rock

When the heart is full ... as in ... full ... and overflowing, the mouth is bereft of words. This is how I felt when I joined the "Mother of all Pilgrimages" ... a pilgrimage to the Holy Land.

As a Catholic Christian I have always looked forward to a religious-themed visit to the venerated sites in Israel and Jordan. These are the places where heaven literally touched earth. This is the land where Jesus, the Son of God, our Savior and Redeemer, was born. This is where He lived, shared His life with others through innumerable healings and other miracles, taught, preached, suffered, died, resurrected, performed miracles after He rose from the dead, ascended into heaven and paved the way for us to follow where He is.

This trip was the journey of the spirit and the soul strengthened with prayers that pierce the heavens. This was a journey of faith that defies understanding and comprehension, of hope that awaits life beyond the here and now, and of love that transcends logic and reason.

Having the opportunity to literally and figuratively walk on the footprints of Jesus, I am at a loss for words to describe an experience that goes beyond the physical state of being.

Perhaps these are the reasons why I find it pointless to even attempt to describe events and experiences during this pilgrimage in a manner similar to my other experiences during other journeys. Each time I sit down and try my hand at writing, I grope for words and I find none. I remain awestruck, dumbfounded, speechless, and wordless. For what can be more futile than to try to confine within a box of finite dimensions that which is infinite in nature?

Lesson learned: *"It is an exercise in futility to describe the indescribable."*

# PEOPLE YOU MEET ALONG THE WAY

Undeniably, a journey has numerous facets.  As I probe more deeply into these various dimensions, I have discovered a very interesting aspect ... an aspect that gives the spark which starts off a long-lasting impression by way of a touch with the unexpected. A very ordinary person, that's me ... coming face to face with extraordinary people is by no means an ordinary experience.

One never knows who one would bump into in the near and far corners of the globe.  These include the famous faces of celebrities who dwell in the limelight, the not-so-famous but great in their own right, the nameless strangers whose lives crossed yours and left a mark, and the infamous faceless whom you would have preferred to stay in the dark.  I have encountered some of them.  In some cases they were expected because I came to see them; in other cases they were unexpected, but fate allowed our paths to cross.

## The Senator

I believe that I was 6 years old at that time; a few years after the Second World War ended.   It was one of those rare occasions when my mother and father brought me to my paternal grandparents' house in Iloilo City for a weekend visit.  A long table laden with festive food has been prepared.  "This is unusual. Something special must be happening.  What could it be?" I thought to myself.

People started arriving.  I was quietly observing them.  I overheard conversations about a  prospective presidential candidate coming to address the group which my aunt has assembled.  She was active in Philippine politics.

Senator Lorenzo Tanada.  That was his name.  My young heart pounded with excitement in anticipation of seeing, hopefully meeting an important personality of our young nation.  I saw him close.  He even gently patted my head!

## The Movie Stars

As a teenager I was fascinated by the fame, popularity and

235

stature of movie stars and stage performers. Two of my classmates and I went to Balara, a park in Quezon City, to watch two
of the most famous movie stars of that time. They were on location shooting episodes of a new movie. Our trip paid off. The
two movie personalities favored us with their autographs and a
pose for pictures. We giggled with excitement! Imagine, ... we
were in the company of Amalia Fuentes and Romeo Vasquez!

This was followed by an unexpected "sighting" of another
prominent movie star, Jose Mari, at the gate of Stella Maris College where my cousin Judith was attending school. We were
honored to shake hands with him.

### The American Show Business Personalities

During the 1960s I was one of the 15,000 people in the audience
screaming with delight at each of the live performances of Nat
King Cole, Johnny Mathis and Pat Boone at the Araneta Coliseum, the biggest dome coliseum in Asia at that time. Oh! How
I swooned over them! They were fantastic superstars. Their
performances exceeded my wildest expectations. To see them
in person was incomprehensible to me! These experiences were
unforgettable.

### The Balladeer

Then there was this famous balladeer, TV personality, song writer and recording artist, Nonoy Zuniga. He was a medical student
at the university where I was teaching. One day on my way to
visit a friend who was a patient at the hospital, I found myself
alone with this celebrity in the elevator. We simply smiled at
each other. He knew that I recognized him. This chance meeting
delighted not only me, but also my friend.

### The Pianist

I was thrilled to listen to Joselito Pascual, one of my favorite
performing and recording pianists during the 1980s. He was
playing at the Manila Hotel. We were seated beside the stage
and he favored us with a warm handshake, a friendly smile and
a picture with him.

## World Renowned Musician

When the Grammy Awardee, Henry Mancini, a world renowned composer, arranger, conductor, concert performer, film and TV musical score writer, musician-par-excellence, performed at the Folk Arts Theater situated at the Philippine Cultural Center Complex in Manila, I joined the standing ovation to honor him after his laudable performance. Watching and listening to his outstanding live performance was a truly memorable experience.

## Pope Paul VI

In November 1970, my late husband and I joined the more than one million throng who attended the open air Mass celebrated at the Quezon City Circle by Pope Paul VI. My husband had to lift up my small frame so that I could see over the crowd so as to catch a glimpse of the Holy Father. I may have been at a considerable distance from His Holiness but, nevertheless, seeing him in person was a treasurable experience.

## Pope John Paul II

I was one of the thousands who lined the campus streets at the University of Santo Tomas to welcome Pope John Paul II during his first visit to the Philippines in 1981. I was an arm's length away from this saintly human being.

At the Vatican I had a second close encounter ... an unexpected one ... with his Holiness Pope John Paul II. It was October 1997. My friend and host in Rome, Dr. Arsol Reyes, Ph.D., had scheduled our attendance at the Sunday Mass at St. Peter's Basilica. We were walking towards the main door of the basilica, admiring the elliptical St. Peter's Square and the colonnade which to me looked like a pair of open arms welcoming and ready to embrace all who enter this holy place. As we neared the obelisk at the center of the square, my musings were broken by my friend's voice, "Evelyn, I wonder what surprise we are in for today. There seems to be an unusual hum of activities." Having been a regular attendee of masses here for almost a year now, I guess she knew of what she spoke.

"You know what? I won't really mind if the Pope himself celebrates our Mass." I responded.

"Wishful thinking! But who knows?"

As soon as we entered the monumental center of Christianity, I felt hypnotized by the awesome baldacchino that accentuates and rises above the Papal Altar. Then we found ourselves in the midst of hundreds of bishops and priests speaking with the American accent.

"Father, what's going on?" I asked.

"The Holy Father is celebrating the Mass for the ongoing Synod of American Bishops."

I turned to Arsol. "Did you hear that? So, this is an extraordinary Sunday for us. I can't believe we're this fortunate!"

We seated ourselves as close as we could to the center aisle. When the Holy Father processed through the aisle, I was privileged to have a close look at his smiling, serene, peaceful, joyful countenance. This was despite his looking bent, weak and frail. When he passed by dispensing his papal blessings, I ceremoniously "caught" his blessings with my right hand and symbolically pressed it to my heart.

On hindsight now, I can declare that once in my lifetime I was blessed by a truly living saint!

## The Prince of the Church

His Eminence Josef Cardinal Glemp was visiting New Jersey. He was scheduled to celebrate Mass at St. Valentine Church in Bloomfield. Being the trustee of our parish in Irvington, my friend Norman S. Karpf was invited to the occasion. As secretary of our Parish Council, I, too, was invited. Without any hesitation we accepted the invitation. It is not a common event to be in the presence of one of the princes of the Roman Catholic hierarchy. To my mind, what made him more special was the fact that Cardinal Glemp came from the same country as the Holy Father, Pope John Paul II.

As expected, the church was packed, mostly with the Cardinal's compatriots from Poland. The celebration was very solemn.

After the Mass, the Cardinal greeted the congregants who approached him. There was a long line of men and women who wanted to greet him. We opted to stay at the back of the line. When our turn came, the Filipino Pastor, Rev. Juancho de Leon, introduced Mr. Karpf and I as parishioners from Irvington. Then referring to me, he added, "Your Eminence, please meet my fellow Filipino."

I reached out my hand to kiss his ring as is the custom in my homeland. I was so thrilled with what was happening that for a moment I forgot where I was. I blurted out a most unusual greeting, "Your Eminence, welcome to the Philippines!" He responded with a broad smile on his face.

My "misplaced" welcome became an ice breaker ... some kind of opening remarks which started a long and animated conversation between the Cardinal and me. "So, you are from the Philippines?" Before I could answer, he continued. "Yes, yes, I have been to your country. Your Cardinal, ... Jaime Cardinal Sin ... yes, Cardinal Sin ... isn't that an ironic name? ... is a very good friend of mine. I immensely enjoyed my visit with him. But I'm sad to learn that he is presently ill." ... He went on and on reminiscing fondly about his trip to the Philippines.

Before we bade goodbye, Mr. Karpf, who was quietly listening to this dialogue, suddenly remarked, "With all due respect to your Eminence, and to you Rev. Juancho, why did Evelyn welcome Cardinal Glemp to the Philippines? Aren't we all in New Jersey? Or have we been suddenly transported to Manila?" The now almost empty church reverberated with our laughter.

**The Basketball Star**

Traveling on the Garden State Parkway of New Jersey on our way to Maryland and Washington D.C., we stopped for a break at one of the rest areas alongside the Parkway. We were playing the game "People Watching" as we sat quietly sipping our iced tea and munching on our chicken nuggets. Soon a lively entourage of what I called "tall people" walked in, sat at a table beside us, got busy with some food, and continued having fun with each other. We eyed them curiously. One of them looked very familiar. "Who is he?" We asked each other.

Then suddenly, recollections of pictures on a sports magazine jumped out of my friend's mind. "See the tallest guy? He's Michael Jordan. The famous superstar of basketball!"

Surreptitiously, I took a picture of him for my nephew who was Michael Jordan's avid fan.

## The Vice President of the United States of America

What better place is there to celebrate Memorial Day but in the most hallowed grounds of the Arlington National Cemetery in Virginia? After a unanimous decision, a group of us Filipinos left New Jersey to be in Arlington National Cemetery for the 1992 celebrations. It was our first visit to this peaceful place of rest for our brave and honored war heroes. During our walk through the headstones, we learned that Vice President Dan Quayle would be the guest of honor at the wreath-laying ceremonies at the Tomb of the Unknown Soldier. Upon learning this, we hurried to the ceremonial area and took our seats as close to the stage as possible.

We patiently waited for his arrival. Then as the solemn ceremonies progressed I could feel the pride welling in my heart ... pride for having immigrated to this "land of the free and home of the brave" ... pride for having the opportunity to celebrate the memories of the brave who keep us free! Add to this the excitement of being in the presence of the second most powerful man in the world; that truly was a memorable Memorial Day!

Memorial Day, 1992, Arlington National Cemetery

## The Courageous Author

We were at Bran Castle, otherwise known as Dracula's Castle in Transylvania, Romania. We were busy exploring every nook and cranny of the ancient structure. When we reached the balcony, our attention suddenly shifted to the beautiful valley be-

240

low. It took some time for Christian, our young handsome and lively Romanian guide, to get our attention. He signaled for us to gather around him. In a hushed tone he asked, "Do you know Salman Rushdie?"

Estela quickly responded. "Do you mean the world famous author of the Satanic Verses whom the Ayatollah Khomeini of Iran ordered to be killed?"

"Sssshhh!" Christian nodded, placed his forefinger to his lips, and continued to whisper. "Yes, the author. Look at the man to your left at the far end of the balcony. That's him."

Our friend Susan rushed towards the unsuspecting Mr. Rushdie for a photograph with him.

We looked and saw a man, no different from us. His greatness is not visible in this setting, but in his fearless writings about sensitive and controversial world-stage issues.

Finding ourselves in the same time and place with this courageous writer is a moment worth remembering.

Susan with Salman Rushdie
at Bran Castle

## The Iconographer

The open museum Etara in Bulgaria was an eye-opener for us who knew very little, if at all, of life in old Bulgaria. The museum specifically shows life in the town of Gabrovo during the 18th and 19th centuries. Our attention was focused upon the Karadzheika water mill which was originally built in 1780. The manner in which they harnessed the power of moving water was unique. Starting with the typical water mill, there was a series of water-driven machineries which were interconnected. This included the weaving loom and their version of the washing machine.

Another interesting feature of this architectural and ethnographic museum is the iconographer's studio. Here we stopped to meet with an iconographer who was busy painting with a form of art which has not changed since ancient times. Pavlina, our Bulgarian guide, introduced us to him. He acknowledged our presence with a nod and a smile. Then he went back to work. As we watched him wordlessly pour his heart and soul to what he was doing, he artfully put the finishing touches to a beautiful icon of the Madonna and Child. Several of his finished masterpieces were exhibited on the walls and shelves in his work room. Some were for sale. As much as we wanted to purchase a piece of his art, it was too pricey for us.

Our visit made me realize the timelessness of art. This gentleman, without any doubt, still bridges the ancient to the present with the skillful work of his artful hands. He is definitely a master of his craft and we were blessed to be in the presence of someone whose work decorates some of the holy places on earth.

**The Numerous Nameless**

There are those numerous nameless people who have left indelible marks in my heart and mind despite the short span of time during which our paths swiftly crossed in the course of our voyages through life. Consider the following:

- the disabled young man (he walked with a severe limp) who carried my heavy wheel-less suitcase a considerable distance from a station in the New York City subway, to the bus at Port Authority, knowing that I had a ride to catch, and that I looked lost in the big city;
- the tour bus driver in Potsdam, Germany who instantly decided that we were all seniors and, without our asking for it, gave us the senior discount for the tour;
- the taxi driver in Beijing, China who, sensing that he was going in the wrong direction, turned off his taxi meter until such time that he found the correct road to the Summer Palace, which was our destination;
- the police officer of Naples, Italy, who, upon learning that

two unescorted Asian women were traveling in the city at night, advised us to keep our gold necklaces out of sight to avoid our being robbed;
- the friar in Padova, Italy, who, upon realizing that we were tourists from a distant land, switched on the lights of the Basilica of St. Justina, the martyr, so that we could see clearly a huge poignant statue of another version of the Pieta;
- the police officer in the highly elevated city of Cusco in Peru who escorted Violy and I to the nearest pharmacy when we told him that we needed medicine for our altitude sickness;
- the elderly gentleman at the Irvington, NJ, bus station who protected me from a drunk when he noticed that the latter was scaring the daylights out of me;
- the group of men in Cappadocia, Turkey who pushed our van back to the pavement thus preventing it from sliding towards the embankment after they saw me jump out in fright;
- a fellow traveler who generously handed me 100.00 Philippine pesos to help me pay for the unexpected airport fee at the Manila International Airport;
- the elderly owner of a vintage 1908 car which was on display in Millburn, NJ, with a huge forbidding sign "Don't Touch!!!" but who allowed me to get up and sit in the driver's seat for a photograph with his car;
- the two elderly ladies who, upon seeing that I was alone on the dome of St. Peter's Basilica in Rome, offered to take several pictures of me ... "to show to the people back home that you did climb up here".

These, and many more, are examples of the kind gestures I experienced from my fellow travelers.

**The Infamous Faceless**

Unfortunately not all is well in this otherwise wonderful world. There are those who remain faceless, not because of humility, but because they have chosen to spread dread and misery on other people's lives. Consider the following:
- the bag slasher / pickpocket just outside ... of all places ... the walls of the sacred Vatican who succeeded in inflicting two long slashes on my bag but ... luckily for me ... was unable

to take anything from it;

- the pickpocket in Madrid who snatched all of Leo's money from his pocket;
- the vendor in Egypt who sold a galabia to Marilou for ten Egyptian pounds, but when handed a U.S.A. fifty dollar bill, gave back forty Egyptian pounds and quickly disappeared;
- the unseen person in Paris who deftly picked Isabel's bag and successfully stole her American Passport.

Despite these negative experiences, essentially it is still a marvelous world! Altogether, the good and the beautiful far outweigh the bad and the ugly.

So ...... keep on traveling! The wonders of the planet await you!

Lesson learned: *"Travel allows one to have a glimpse of a wider spectrum of the human race."*

# DISRUPTION

Our pace quickened as we approached the white marble balcony in front of the Tomb of the Unknown Soldier at Arlington National Cemetery in Virginia. It was two minutes before 11:00 a.m. The steps facing the tomb were all taken by anxious spectators. The solemn-faced crowd looked comfortably seated despite the scorching 98 degree summer heat.

My nephew Jopet was visiting Virginia for the first time. This trip was part of his gift for having recently graduated with a Bachelor's degree in Nursing from the Prairie View A & M University, and for having successfully passed the State Board Examination immediately thereafter. This young man is now a registered nurse. This was his first visit to the hallowed grounds of Arlington, the final resting place of America's finest and bravest men and women.

Aside from Jopet and I, our entourage included my sister Elena, my daughter Rosanne and my granddaughter Kiara.

The shaded left hand corner of the balcony beckoned us. A few people were already seated on the floor. We joined them. We sat under the refreshing shade of the bushes. Everyone was glued to their seats in anticipation of the solemn ceremonies. At exactly 11:00 a.m., with expected military punctuality, the ceremonial Changing of the Guard commenced. Except for the soft clicking of the cameras and the sharp snapping click of the soldiers' shoes, you could hear a pin drop. The crowd was respectfully and politely silent. All eyes were on the soldiers in their crisp uniforms, with their perfectly polished shoes, shining buttons and buckles, and gleaming rifles. All of these enhanced the dignified military posture, the clean-cut look and the precise movements of the military personnel who serve as honor guards over the graves.

For a brief moment a military command cut through the silent crowd. Then, once again, complete silence befell the audience. No one moved from their seats. The only discernible movements among the crowd were their heads turning left or right following the soldiers as they marched across the balcony. From where we were seated, only our eyes moved.

It was at this moment when two women and a man, all late comers, walked right across in front of me. The women went to the side and stood beside the balustrade. The man stood right in front of me, thus completely blocking my view.

"Please sit down." I whispered. He did not budge. "Please sit down." I softly repeated.

Without an iota of courtesy he murmured, "Soon you will be asked to stand anyway."

"Yes, but that will be later on." I responded in a whisper. What I really wanted to say was: "You rude, uneducated, uncouth, uncivilized moron, which planet did you come from?"

Just as I finished silently venting my anger his cell phone rang, disrupting the solemn silence among the crowd. His profanity further disrupted the peace. His hand desperately searched through his multi-pocketed shirt and knee-length summer attire. He caught the culprit phone, flipped it open and hurriedly spoke in a foreign language to the caller while sprinting out of my way.

Without much thought, he sat beside a sign, so clearly displayed, that even eyes clouded by cataract could plainly see. "Do not sit on, stand on or cross the rail." He simply ignored the sign.

Lesson learned: *"Some people behave like a black spot on an otherwise plain white sheet. Let it not be you!"*

# A HUMBLING EXPERIENCE

Sunrise over the Nile

Someone once said, "Traveling is a humbling experience."

I couldn't quite grasp that concept the first time I came across that quotation. ... Neither did I understand it for a long time. But after having traveled extensively through 39 different countries in the five continents of North America, South America, Europe, Asia and Africa, and having visited 29 of the 50 states in the United States, ... and still counting ... , I can now pretty much say that I have somehow grasped the essence of that philosophical thought.

I have become more fully aware of how limited and insignificant is my knowledge of anything ... of everything ... , and how enormous are the experiences out there which captivate my interest and which compel me to learn and to try to understand them. Now I somehow realize these facts because I have touched, felt, heard, seen, and even tasted them. Almost mystically I consciously recognize how small indeed I am compared to the grandiosity of great men and women and their almost immortal achievements.

I have learned that although ... "a picture can paint a thousand words", or perhaps a movie presentation can evoke a million more words, neither can capture the ecstatic feeling I had when my heart seemed to jump out as I caught sight of the magical fleeting moment when the brilliant orange sun, rising over the Nile River, showed its double reflection on the river's bend as I watched it from a hot air balloon a thousand feet above.

Neither can it capture that "Wow moment" when hiking up the terraces in Machu Picchu, Peru we reached that level where our guide told us to look back and then right before me was the panoramic view of the enormous astounding Incan City.

My travels have humbled me by making me learn, and hence, correct many of my own misconceptions.

For instance my idea of an oasis was a small spring bubbling out of the desert sand surrounded by a dozen or so palm trees. That was the picture I saw in some books. Call me naive or even ignorant, but it was not until I visited the Holy Land and in particular the City of Jericho did I learn that an oasis could encompass a whole city. Jericho is an oasis city fed by myriad springs gushing out its life-giving waters to a vast area of an otherwise barren earth.

I have read about glaciers chipping off. I thought it was a thin sheet of ice placidly chipping off and melting away. Not 'till I traveled to Alaska and heard a thunderous boom and watched a chunk of ice as big as a mansion crack and splash into the water, did I know full well how big a "chip" that was.

Pictures of the Walls of China are commonly seen decorating the walls of Chinese restaurants. I know it's pretty. But what's so out-of-this-world about it? It was not until I walked on the Wall itself that I grasped the immensity of its magnitude, the width, the length, the sturdiness, the durability, the elegance of the structure, and the precarious locations on which most parts of it stand. It stretches beyond one's imagination.

I've read about and seen a multitude of pictures of Michelangelo's Sistine Chapel. But it wasn't until I stared wide-eyed, mouth-gaping, heart-thumping, neck-breaking, did I finally get awestruck at such a heavenly work of art... an extraordinary achievement by a giant of a man!

As children we read about ages ago ... "Once upon a time ... ." " ... and then the bad guy was thrown into the dungeon to rot in the dark and the cold." This sounded like unreal to me. Not until I saw ruins of numerous castles did I feel the shivers up and

248

down my spine, sensed something creeping through my skin, and felt like throwing up in utter disgust to realize that these dungeons did exist in castles that were real and active in their time.

Rila Monastery

There were times  when we visted a place without any preconceived idea of what we would find.  Upon reaching our destination, I was profoundly  humbled by the beauty and elegance of the structures, paintings, statues, sculptures, and decorations made by hands endowed with artistic gifts.  These we saw in the Rila Monastery deep in the wooded mountains of Bulgaria as well as along the streets of Riga in Latvia.  In the former, I gazed in speechless wonder at the artfully designed colorful icons which covered every inch of the monastery chapel.  In the latter I was astonished and overwhelmed by the marvelous Nouveau Art designs presented on every building along the main avenues of the old city.

The more I see and wonder at both the natural and man-made splendor throughout the world, the more conscious I become of my insignificant role on this planet.

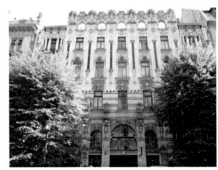

Nouveau Art in Riga

Lesson Learned: *"Traveling, without an iota of doubt, is truly a humbling experience."*

# JUST AROUND THE CORNER

Oftentimes when we set our sights to great distances, we miss what is just around the corner.

The magnificent Cathedral Basilica of the Sacred Heart in Newark, New Jersey is a stone's throw from where I reside. It is the fifth largest cathedral in North America. It was granted the status of Basilica by Pope John Paul II during his visit to Newark in October 1995.

Cathedral Basilica of the
Sacred Heart, Newark, NJ

Despite its proximity, it took me 17 years to fully appreciate the magnificence of this French Gothic architectural structure whose 323 foot towers and great copper spire dominate the landscape. Its dignified appearance is further enhanced by the formidable yet welcoming main door; the finely crafted stained glass and rose windows; the marble walls, columns and floors; the intricate wood paneling; and the crystal chandeliers. It surpasses some of the more famous cathedrals of Europe.

Invited to attend the Easter Sunday Mass of 2006, the Basilica captivated me. The solemnity of the Mass celebrated by Archbishop John Joseph Myers, together with the overpowering vocal renditions by the renowned Cathedral Choir, was spiritually uplifting. From that time on my Easter and Christmas masses are always celebrated here at this Basilica.

Lesson learned: *"Even as you set your eyes afar, there could also be something astounding just around the corner."*

# ABOUT THE AUTHOR

*Just as the lifestyle on the man-made islands of Lake Titikaka is worlds apart from the lifestyle on the island of Manhattan, so is technical writing as in the writing of textbooks and references with the rigid accuracy of the exact science of mathematics, worlds apart from literary writing which is made colorful by the interplay of senses and emotions. Yet somehow, for some inexplicable reason, these two very different worlds are both manifested in the writings of the author. A gentle touch of philosophical insights has also given much depth to her book.*

*Although as a child she dreamed of being a writer, a twist of fate thrust her into the technical world of engineering. Yet her late father's words of wisdom spoken to her more than six decades ago kept her dream alive: "You can earn a degree in engineering and still be a writer, but you cannot earn a degree in journalism and be an engineer."*

*Like Rip van Winkle who woke from a deep slumber after two decades, so, too, her slumbering passion for literary writing was awoken by decades of traveling through time, distant places, and the many phases of life.*

*Evelina Jara Masaoy is a widowed mother of six, a grandmother of nine, and a great grandmother of one. In addition to having a large family, she lays claim to a few very close friends, numerous acquaintances and a growing number of traveling companions.*

*Before immigrating to the U.S.A. in 1989, she was a Chemical Engineering professor at the Royal and Pontifical University of Santo Tomas (UST), Manila, Philippines, for 26 years. During that period she was also a Lecturer at numerous Engineering Review Centers.*

*She graduated from the UST with a degree of B.S. in Chemical Engineering, magna cum laude, and earned a Masters Degree in Engineering, Chemical Engineering Education from the University of the Philippines, Quezon City, Philippines. She has co-authored a textbook in College Algebra; several reference books in Engineering Mathematics which include College Algebra, Trigonometry, Analytic Geometry, Differential Calculus and Integral Calculus; and a Review Manual in Electronics and Communications Engineering designed as a guide to prepare for Government Licensure Examinations.*

*Shifting from technical writing to literary essays, she honed her skills by serving as the Editor-in-Chief of the official Newsletter of the University of Santo Tomas Engineering Alumni Association in the U.S.A. for almost ten years. She was also the Secretary of this association whose main goal is to provide scholarship grants to gifted but needy engineering students at her alma mater. In January 2012 she became Co-President of the association.*

*As Parish Council Secretary of St. Leo Church, Irvington, New Jersey, she was also a contributor to Leo's Lines, the parish newsletter, edited by the pastor, Rev. Thomas M. Cembor.*

*She serves as a lector at St. Michael Church, Union, New Jersey, in which township she resides.*

*She is employed as an Analytical Chemist in a New Jersey environmental laboratory.*

*The Author with Archbishop John Joseph Myers at the Cathedral Basillica of the Sacred Heart, Newark, at the Easter Mass of 2006

*This photograph was published in the Archdiocesan Newspaper, The Catholic Advocate, in 2006 and again in 2011.

The Wonders of Wandering
P.O. Box 5028
Hillside, New Jersey 07205